THE REAL BASIL BROWN

FROM RICKINGHALL TO SUTTON HOO AND BACK

SARAH DOIG

Quatrefoil, 2023

RECORDING LOCAL HISTORY

No 1		A Suffolk Boy in East Africa
No 2		A Walk Through Botesdale - Diana Maywhort
No 3		St Mary's Church, Rickinghall Inferior - Jean Sheehan
No 4		A Walk Through Rickinghall - Diana Maywhort
No 5		Reflections on Redgrave Part 1 - Jean Sheehan
No 6		Victorian and Edwardian Rectors of Rickinghall - Sarah Doig
No 7		Reflections on Redgrave Part 2 - Jean Sheehan
No 8		Botesdale Medieval Market - Diana Maywhort
No 9		Lest We Forget: Botesdale, Redgrave and Rickinghall Men of the Great War - Diana Maywhort and Deborah Wells
No 10		Villages in Wartime: Life in Botesdale, Redgrave and Rickinghall in World War Two - Graham Clayton
No 11		A Rural Education: The History of Schooling in Botesdale, Redgrave and Rickinghall - Sarah Doig
No 12		James Scarfe of Botesdale: One of the Noble Six Hundred - Brian Chandler
No 13		Arthur's Airings: Tales of Botesdale, Redgrave and Rickinghall 1930-2016 - Arthur Bryant
No 14		Shops and Shopping: Four Hundred Years of Retailing in Botesdale, Redgrave and Rickinghall – Graham Clayton
No 15		Portraits of Village Life: Photographs in and around Botesdale, Redgrave and Rickinghall
No 16		The Real Basil Brown: From Rickinghall to Sutton Hoo and back – Sarah Doig

Published by Quatrefoil
4 The Old School, Rickinghall, Suffolk, IP22 1HD
ISBN 978-0-9931706-5-2
© Quatrefoil, 2023

Printed by Gipping Press, Needham Market

All rights reserved. This publication may not be reproduced, stored in a retrieval system, or transmitted, in any form or by any means, electronic, mechanical, photocopying, recording or otherwise, without prior permission of the publisher.

Contents

Illustrations		ii
Acknowledgements		iv
The Basil Brown Archive		vi
Abbreviations		viii
Introduction		ix
1.	Boyhood and Schooldays	1
2.	Farming	7
3.	First Archaeological Forays	19
4.	Employment	31
5.	The Sutton Hoo Years	43
6.	The War Years	69
7.	Peacetime	83
8.	The Brown School of Archaeology	95
9.	Retirement	115
10.	Legacy	137
Bibliography		144

Illustrations

Basil with his bicycle	x
Willow Cottage, Rickinghall	2
Basil at Rickinghall National School	2
Basil's certificates	8
Basil's RAMC certificate of service	10
Basil in RAMC uniform	11
May Brown	13
Basil with his astronomical instruments	16
Basil, May and Mr Armenter	16
Basil in Rickinghall schoolhouse	20
Royal Insurance Company agency sign on Cambria	20
Stubbings Entry, Burgate	23
Cross found at West Street Farm	24
Roman roads in Rickinghall	28
Basil at Calke Wood	33
The Wattisfield skeleton	36
Stanton Chare Roman villa excavation	39
Spoil heaps from Sutton Hoo tumulus 2(D)	45
Sutton Hoo tumulus 4(E)	45
1938 Sutton Hoo finds	46
The tumuli at Sutton Hoo	49
Basil's watercolours of Sutton Hoo tumulus 1(I)	51
The Great Ship Burial	54
The Great Ship Burial	55
Basil at Sutton Hoo	59
The Woodbridge to Sutton ferry	61
Mr & Mrs Cannell and May Brown at Sutton Hoo	61
Basil during or just after the war	71

The first West Stow excavations	76
The first West Stow excavations	77
Basil's wartime scrapbook	79
Basil's wartime scrapbook	80
The Botesdale Roman kiln	85
Basil and Dr Stanley West at West Stow	88
Experimental kiln firing at Calke Wood	91
Plan of the Lady Chapel at Rickinghall Superior Church	96
Finds at Rickinghall Superior Church	97
May Brown	100
Redgrave Hall Tudor doorway	102
The Botesdale Grammar School bell	103
Carvings in Rickinghall Inferior Church	105
English Delft scent bottle	108
Basil in the 1960s	111
Basil at the Facon's Hall dig	116
Basil and his sheds	119
The interior of one of Basil's sheds	120
Basil at home	124
Basil and his helpers at Broom Hills	127
Basil's tent at Broom Hills	127
Records of the Broom Hills dig	128
Basil at Broom Hills	130
Basil and Mr Edwardson	133
The 2007 Basil Brown exhibition	139
The 2009 memorial service	139
Basil's blue plaque mounting in 2023	143

Acknowledgements

There are numerous people who have contributed to this book in various ways. But it simply would not have been able to be written without the help and support of Jean Sheehan and Di Maywhort. Both are enthusiastic and hard-working local historians who have, over the years, collected almost anything they could about Basil Brown. In 2007, Jean and Di organised an exhibition in Rickinghall Inferior Church to celebrate Basil Brown's life and work. They encouraged those locals who remembered Basil and his wife to write down their memories. I have used anonymised snippets from these recollections in this biography, apart from a few individuals from whom I have obtained permission to quote them.

I am also extremely grateful to Julie Kennard and Faye Minter, the custodians of the archives of the Suffolk County Council Archaeological Service. Not only did they allow me access to their Basil Brown Archive hard copy holdings, but they also enabled me to continue work on this book at home during the Coronavirus pandemic by providing me with scanned, digital copies of many of Basil's notebooks. Their support and enthusiasm for my project is much appreciated by all the Quatrefoil team.

Another person instrumental in helping me make this book so complete is Peter Christie who, as a boy and young man, got to know Basil well. He was a regular visitor to the Browns' home in Rickinghall and when Peter moved away from the area, he and Basil kept in touch. After Basil died, his widow, May, gave Peter many of Basil's more personal items such as photographs. Peter has kindly allowed me to use this material in this book making it far more authoritative.

I have also made use of a school project kindly given to us by Martin Chilvers, a local lad who was educated at Culford School. The project, put together in 1968-9, is the result of information the schoolboy gleaned from various talks he had with Basil Brown. It is therefore an invaluable source of accurate facts about Basil's life.

Thank you also to Jack Clark, Collections & House Officer at Sutton Hoo, who enthusiastically facilitated my research visit and subsequent questions.

I would also like to thank the team of archivists at Suffolk Archives, who kindly allowed me to view some of Basil Brown's uncatalogued notebooks.

Another valuable source of information about Basil Brown's later life is the set of the recordings masterminded by Jonathan Abson of The Sutton Hoo Society. They are the result of interviews conducted by Jonathan in 2011 with people who had known Basil. Some of these people are sadly no longer with us. Thank you also to Jonathan Abson, Sue Emerson and Sally Green who patiently transcribed these many hours of interviews. It has certainly made my job of quoting from them far easier. Where I do quote from the interviews, these words are attributed to the respective interviewees who gave their permission at the time for their input to be used at a later date.

Thank you also to Dr Stanley West who has allowed me to draw on his recollections of Basil Brown. The family of Revd Ivan E Moore also kindly provided a relevant extract from his memoirs. I am grateful to Chris and Marcia Bell for providing me with first-hand accounts of Basil Brown from Peggy Healey (née Fellingham) and Arthur "Tinker" Francis. There are several other people who provided photographs and permission to publish them in this book. All images in the book, where possible, are attributed to the photographer or owner.

I am very grateful to my husband, Mike Doig, and Di Maywhort who acted as proof-readers during the whole process of writing and publishing this book. Thank you also to Jean Sheehan for reading through, and commenting on, my drafts, as well as Bob and Jane Carr who cast two pairs of expert archaeological eyes over the draft text.

The Basil Brown Archive

In researching and writing this biography, I have made extensive use of a collection which I describe as the Basil Brown Archive. By this I mean the handwritten notebooks, diaries, scrapbooks, books of newspaper cuttings, photographs, maps, letters from Basil's various correspondents, as well as other written material created and kept by Basil Brown himself throughout his life. Rather than existing as a collection in one place, though, the material is scattered between several different institutions and, in some cases, are in private hands (Basil having generously given away some of his papers of interest to his friends).

Basil Brown's notebooks are many and varied in shape and length, ranging from around a dozen to over 200 pages. There is a series of excavation notebooks and dig diaries in which Basil meticulously recorded every detail of all his digs, including numerous sketches and scale drawings of sites and finds. They also contain photographs of the digs. Many of the other notebooks are full of Basil's painstaking research into local history. There are also site registers and corresponding annotated Ordnance Survey maps which Basil created as part of his Suffolk archaeological reporting role for the Ipswich Museum. In later life, Basil Brown kept notes of daily work, visits and events in desk diaries, some of which survive, and which provide researchers with a more personal insight into his life. All this material is supplemented by two card indexes of finds and copies of Basil's weekly, typewritten reports to the Ipswich Museum. These reports cover the period 1936 to 1961 and record archaeological activity across the county.

On Basil's death in 1977, his archive initially remained with his widow, May. That said, we know that some, probably more personal, papers were understandably destroyed by May. An individual who still has some of Basil's personal effects told me: "When Basil died in March 1977, I was shocked and came home to express my condolences to May. I arrived to find her in the garden stoking up a large bonfire of letters sent to Basil over the previous fifty years. I saved what I could." So, some of what might be classed as part of the Basil Brown archive remains in trusted, private hands. In 1984, a year after May's death, Dr Stanley West, Director of the Suffolk Archaeology Unit (SAU), was contacted by May's solicitor who was disposing of the many papers and archaeological finds which were then still in the Browns' house in Rickinghall. Dr West visited the house and retrieved various of Basil's records and finds for safekeeping by the SAU (now the Suffolk County Council Archaeological Service (SCCAS)). Under the terms of Basil's will, all his diaries relating to his digs at Sutton Hoo were given to the British Museum, where they remain. A further, smaller collection of miscellaneous documents, letters and photos of Basil's are held by The National Trust at Sutton Hoo.

The majority of the Basil Brown Archive has, in recent years, been deposited by the SCCAS in the Suffolk Archives where the material can be held in up-to-date archival storage conditions in The Hold in Ipswich. Some of this collection is available to researchers (under the catalogue reference HD 3096) whilst the bulk of the material deposited by the SCCAS sadly remains uncatalogued (at the time of writing in the summer of 2023) and so these volumes merely bear a generic accession number (18855) until such time as they can be catalogued. In some of the notebooks, there are two sets of page numbering; one by Basil himself and one, presumably, made by the SCCAS. Because of this, and the fact that a small number of volumes have been digitised and are available to view on PDF format (and therefore have a further, different page numbering system) in the Suffolk Archives, I have not referenced page numbers within the volumes.

It should also be noted that the volume numbers were allocated by the SCCAS sometime after they acquired the collection: they are not Basil Brown's own. The numbering system does not follow a chronological sequence of Basil's record-keeping.

Abbreviations

NT	The National Trust
SA/B	Suffolk Archives, Bury St Edmunds
SA/I	Suffolk Archives, Ipswich
SCCAS	Suffolk County Council Archaeological Service
SH	Sutton Hoo
TNA	The National Archives

Introduction

Today, although Basil Brown is not a household name, he is widely recognised and respected in archaeological circles for his discovery, on the eve of the Second World War, of the Anglo-Saxon Great Ship Burial at Sutton Hoo. More recently, the Netflix film *The Dig*, based on John Preston's novel of the same name, has served to introduce the wider public to Basil's key role in the successful excavation. Back in 1951, though, there was no mention of Basil at all in the large display about the Sutton Hoo treasure at the Festival of Britain. However, in recent years this injustice Basil felt in having been almost completely "airbrushed" out of the story has been rectified. He now, quite rightly, takes centre stage at the exhibition in Tranmer House at The National Trust's Sutton Hoo site. In Rickinghall, his home for practically all the eighty-nine years of his life, and in the neighbouring villages too, Basil has always been held in the highest regard, and is fondly and proudly remembered.

This biography is an attempt to tell the story of the real Basil Brown, including his life and achievements from a local perspective. It uses Basil's own words wherever possible to demonstrate his motivations, passions and discoveries. I also draw heavily, especially for his later life, on recollections from people who knew him, some of whom owe a debt of gratitude to Basil for introducing them to history and archaeology. I have not detailed all Basil's many archaeological digs and investigations across Suffolk. It would be an impossible task to cover his lifetime's work in a single volume such as this, and it would not do Basil's accomplishments due justice. Instead, I have concentrated on various of his excavations in Rickinghall and the surrounding area. I have, of course, covered the Sutton Hoo years, but from a more personal angle than previous books on Basil's dig have done. The result is, I hope, a readable yet informative picture of the man who made one of the most significant archaeological discoveries of all time and for whom, having studied his numerous notebooks and diaries, I have the greatest admiration.

Basil with his bicycle – undated but probably late 1900s or early 1910s (SCCAS)

Chapter 1
Boyhood and Schooldays

"My imagination may have been a little gilt edged"

Basil Brown was, unquestionably, a Rickinghall man. Apart from the first few months, he lived all his life in the two parishes of Rickinghall Inferior and Rickinghall Superior. Basil John Wait Brown was born in Bucklesham near Ipswich on 22 January 1888 and was the only child of George Brown, then a wheelwright, and his wife Charlotte (née Wait).[1] George Brown came from a Suffolk farming family and had grown up in Burgate where his father, John, was a farm bailiff. Basil's mother had been born in Great Barrington, Gloucestershire and had worked as a domestic servant before marrying.

It is highly likely that the Browns' move in 1888 to Rickinghall was for employment on Church Farm, under the farmer, George Gooderham: the same census shows one of George Brown's nieces, Agnes, working as a domestic servant in the Gooderham household. At that time, the Brown family group was headed by Basil's grandfather, John, who died in 1890.

In 1891, when the national decennial census was taken, the adjoining parishes of Rickinghall Inferior and Rickinghall Superior had a total population of around 950. It was a rural community dominated by agriculture. Those not employed on farms were mainly self-employed tradesmen and craftsmen. Basil's family were recorded in the census living in Stow Road in Rickinghall Superior. It was his 71-year-old widowed grandmother, Harriet Brown, who was listed as the head of the household together with her son, George, his wife and the 3-year-old Basil. Harriet's occupation is recorded as a farmer. George is described as a labourer.

Although the 1891 census does not record exactly where the Browns' house was, Martin Chilvers' school project includes a colour photograph of a house near Rickinghall Superior Church. He captions this: "The cottage in Rickinghall where Mr Brown lived as a boy. In those days the roof was thatched." This property is now known as Willow Cottage.

Willow Cottage as it looked when Basil lived there (Courtesy of Geoffrey Mayhew)

Basil – front row, 3rd from right – at the age of six (Courtesy of Peter Christie)

Like many other farmers, George Gooderham held the tenancy of Church Farm, rather than owning it outright. He had taken over the tenancy from his father, William, who, in 1861, farmed 186 acres. Although they did not own the farm buildings and land, such tenant farmers owned their own farm stock, implements and machinery. After his death, when George Gooderham's farm stock was sold off, it included nine horses, a bull, thirteen dairy cows, ten beef cattle, twenty-seven pigs and some fowl.[2]

As a general labourer on the farm, George Brown, would have been expected to turn his hand to a number of agricultural tasks, although his wheelwrighting skills were no doubt used on the various farm carts. The young Basil, according to Martin Chilvers' school project, helped his father on the farm from a very early age. Martin records: "In those days his mother helped by making butter in the dairy. She also brewed very good wine, according to Basil. Then farming was a family job, everyone helping in some way or another."

The young scholar
At the age of five, Basil started attending the local Rickinghall National School in Hinderclay Road. This had been founded in 1853 by the then Rector and was established as a Church of England school. At around the time of Basil's admission into the infant class in 1893, there were about 150 pupils at the school. Alongside attendance figures, special activities and events, the surviving school logbook covering this period records details of the curriculum covered by the teachers.[3] In addition to the "3 Rs" - reading, writing and arithmetic - the children learned geography, history and natural history, as well drawing and music.

In 1899, the headteacher, Charles Canham, noted in the logbook that the school had received a new map of the world and had also acquired ten sheets of object lessons with actual specimens. Object lessons had become compulsory in 1895 for younger pupils and consisted of bringing into the classroom either natural or man-made objects, each of which would form the basis for a lesson. Religious education was taught by the Rector, Revd George Hales, and his Curate, Revd Edmund Farrer, was also a frequent visitor.

School life in a rural community such as Rickinghall was also, inevitably, affected by the farming year. The school logbook is littered with entries recording children, more often than not the older boys, being absent from their lessons helping in the fields at crucial times. In fact, the summer school holiday was dictated by the farming year. In 1894, the headmaster recorded: "Broke up school on 10 August for Harvest holidays and returned 6 weeks later."

In 1967, a local newspaper printed a Rickinghall School photo dating from 1894 with the following comment: "When this picture was taken some 73 years ago at Rickinghall School, it is doubtful whether the young lad third from the right in the front row could spell archaeology or knew what it meant. But today he is acknowledged as one of the leading authorities in local history in north Suffolk and south Norfolk. His name? Basil Brown. And he lent me this picture a few days ago. Mr Brown, who was younger than most of those on the photograph, was able to name his contemporaries in the front row - left to right: Robert Ray, Richard Cook, Ethel Cook, Anna Rowsher, himself, Charles Shemming and Tom Rush. Mr Edward Canham was the teacher, and his wife is also in the picture."

Very few entries in the logbook record pupils' names and so we know very little about how the young Basil performed and behaved in class. The only entry in which he is named is on 15 May 1901 when the following is recorded: "The Revd S Aldwell gave prizes to the children who passed the best examination in Religious Knowledge - 1st Prize A Hazell, 2nd Prize Basil Brown, 3rd Prize Eva Wilby." Basil Brown gave this interesting, brief insight into his schooldays recorded by Martin Chilvers: "He distinctly remembers disliking history, waiting to prove his teacher wrong at every possible opportunity."

A thirst for knowledge
Basil's desire to learn apparently started at an early age. He talked about how his interest in astronomy started at the age of five, saying: "My grandfather was interested in it and I got hold of some of his old books and charts."[4] Martin Chilvers writes in his project: "Right from his childhood Basil's interests have been archaeology and astronomy ... he would often dig and dig and see what he could find and when it was too dark, he would watch the stars." Basil Brown records, in his *Suffolk Explorations*, of

growing up with stories of hoards of gold coins being unearthed at Helmingham, where his father's family came from. Basil writes: "My grandmother's accounts of finds used to fan my boyhood coin collecting, exploring propensities etc. So perhaps on my several excursions along this route my imagination may have been a little gilt edged."[5]

Basil Brown told both the newspapers and Martin Chilvers that, like other boys at the time, he had received private tutoring in addition to his day schooling. We know no more about the nature of this supplementary education, nor do we know who his tutor or tutors were.[6] Even if he was not one of his formal tutors, Revd Edmund Farrer influenced Basil's passion for history and archaeology. In his *Suffolk Explorations*, Basil writes of the "various interesting talks I had with him."

Basil also acknowledges help from Farrer in his book, *Astronomical Atlases, Charts and Maps*.[7] Revd Farrer moved on from his Rickinghall curacy in 1896 to neighbouring Hinderclay where he was the Rector until 1915, and so it is highly likely that Basil continued contact with the clergyman to try to satisfy his voracious appetite for learning. Farrer contributed regular articles on local and general history for "East Anglian Miscellany" which appeared in the *East Anglian Daily Times* from 1901 and some of these appear pasted into Basil's notebooks and scrapbooks.

It is possible that another of Basil's informal tutors, although most probably when Basil was a young man, was Revd Henry Kingsmill Brown. The clergyman was Rector of Rickinghall Inferior and Superior from 1913 until 1936. According to a former local resident, Basil used to help in the rector's garden and Revd Brown apparently taught him a lot, including Latin.

One rather nice fact gleaned from surviving copies of the *Rickinghall Magazine* is that Basil sang as a boy in the Rickinghall Superior church choir.[8] The run of these magazines is not complete but from the issues that exist, Basil served as a boy chorister from May 1898 until September 1902. By this time, he was approaching his fifteenth birthday and so it is likely that his days as a boy treble were, in any case, numbered.

According to Martin Chilvers' school project, Basil left school at the age of twelve. However, the school prizegiving entry in the logbook from May

1901 suggests that Basil may have stayed on until the summer of that year, when he would have been thirteen. This is confirmed by Basil's mention, in his reminiscences on astronomy, of Mrs Hartree as his temporary headteacher.[9] Annie Hartree took temporary charge of the school from March to June 1901 during the illness, and after the death, of Charles Canham. The compulsory school leaving age at the time was twelve and so it is possible that Basil had persuaded his father that he might extend his formal education. However, Basil would certainly have had responsibilities helping on the farm when not in the schoolroom and, as Martin records: "The day after he [Basil] left school he started to work on the farm."

---

[1] Basil's birth certificate records "Waite" rather than "Wait" but we know from numerous other records that the latter was the usual spelling.
[2] *East Anglian Daily Times* 15 September 1908, page 3.
[3] Rickinghall National School logbook 1891-1919 (SA/B: ADB 540/1/3).
[4] *Daily Express* 15 January 1935.
[5] *Suffolk Explorations* is an unfinished (or partly lost) typescript manuscript written by Basil Brown and now held by the SSCAS.
[6] Chris Durrant mentions two, unnamed retired clergymen.
[7] Brown, Basil, J W *Astronomical Atlases, Charts and Maps: An Historical and General Guide* (Search Publishing Co., London, 1932).
[8] In private hands.
[9] See page 7.

Chapter 2
Farming

"My wish was to be an astronomer"

The end of Basil Brown's formal schooling, probably sometime in 1901, marked the beginning of his life-long drive for self-improvement and passion for learning about all things natural and physical. So, when not helping on the farm alongside his parents, Basil was studying either on his own or through opportunities for study for those above school age.

Studying in his spare time
Rickinghall National School had a well-established night school which, according to the logbooks, had started in 1866.[1] These evening classes were for married and single young men and boys who had left school but who wanted to continue their studies. By 1895, the night school had fifty-three people enrolled in these classes, although by the early twentieth century, attendance had levelled out at between twenty and thirty mature students. The local parish magazine reports that in the 1890s, evening school sessions included arithmetic, letter writing, English, composition, reading, geography and drawing. The East Suffolk Technical Council examined the attendees and a surviving certificate issued by this body tells us that Basil attended the evening school in 1902 and passed an examination - second class - in drawing; a skill he used to good effect throughout his life.[2]

Although we don't know whether Basil studied subjects other than drawing at the night school, he spent as much time as possible studying, on his own, various subjects in which he took a particular interest. In one of his notebooks, Basil records:
"In 1901 and following years I was helped in my studies by Mrs Hartree (the Headteacher at Rickinghall School during the illness of Mr Canham the Headmaster). Mrs Hartree took an interest in astronomy and helped me, I remember, after a lesson in which the scholars were asked to write what they would like to be, my wish was to be an astronomer and view the stars through a telescope. Though perhaps a professional astronomer was meant, I have been able to get much pleasure from a study of the stars as an amateur with a small telescope. There have been

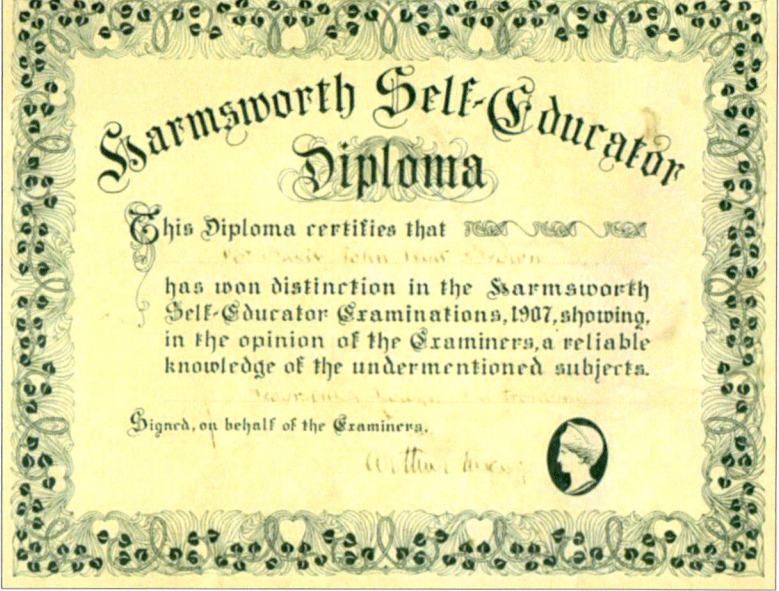

Basil's Evening School and Harmsworth Self-Educator certificates (SCCAS)

intervals during which I have not taken so much interest in astronomy, but have returned after a time to this study. In 1907 I was given a diploma for my paper in which the questions answered were set by the editor of the Harmsworth Self Educator. This diploma was for geography, geology and astronomy."[3]

Indeed, the survival of Basil's diploma certificate in a bundle of his personal papers is testament to how proud he was to have achieved this level of education.[4] The Harmsworth Self-Educator was an educational magazine series, published in forty-eight issues between 1905 and 1907. In the introduction to the first instalment, the editor wrote: "The Harmsworth Self-Educator is designed to be a working school of life. Its purpose is to lay the foundations of an adaptable and successful career for the thousands of young men and women who are bewildered by the increasing difficulty of choosing a definite aim in life, or, having a definite aim, of adapting themselves to its conditions."[5] The emphasis was on practical subjects of use to the various professions and ranged from languages, agriculture, beekeeping and gardening, to materials & structures, leather and woodworking.

Another indication of Basil's thirst for knowledge is an interesting, surviving set of scrapbooks kept by him, two of which date from the first few decades of the twentieth century.[6] Newspaper and magazine cuttings range from countermarks on ancient coins, new astronomical discoveries, archaeological explorations (including the recent discovery of the tomb of Tutankhamen), postage stamps, aspects of arable and livestock farming, flora and fauna (especially birds) through to weather phenomena and rare books. They show the sheer breadth of Basil's interests. A particular interest, throughout his life, was in the Roman era and an early notebook is full of sketches made by Basil of Roman emperors.[7]

Church Farm
We do not know exactly when Basil's father, George, took over the tenancy of Church Farm. Local directory entries up to 1908 record George Brown as a farmer and wheelwright. His living was a precarious one, with a wife, son and mother (until her death in 1906) to feed. So, in 1889, George also became an agent for the Royal Insurance Company, selling life and fire insurance to local residents for which he received commission on any new

Basil's First World War volunteer force certificate (SCCAS)

Basil in RAMC uniform in 1918/19 (© National Trust / Archie Donald Maling)

or renewed policies he signed up.[8] His employer, George Gooderham, died in August 1907 and a year later the late farmer's farmstock, carriage, farm implements and some of his household furniture was sold by his widow at auction.[9]

It is therefore possible that this is when the Browns moved into Church Farm to take over the running of this relatively small farm. George Brown's wife, Charlotte, as well as Basil, who was by now in his twenties, would have been expected to help out with all manner of work, be it tending to the livestock or trying to farm the arable land. In November 1915, an alleged nuisance at Church Farm was discussed at a meeting of the Hartismere Rural District Council. There had clearly been complaints from neighbours about the noise from the farm's pigs. A solution was happily found: the piggery was moved from its position adjoining the passageway of the cottages to a more distant location![10]

Basil spent most of the First World War at Church Farm in Rickinghall, helping his parents. On 22 November 1915, Basil had presented himself at the recruitment office at Eye with the intention of signing up to serve in the Army Reserve for the duration of the war. However, his surviving enlistment form is simply endorsed "Not accepted Medically Unfit".[11] Sadly, we do not know why he was turned down: no records survive of unsuccessful applications. Photographs of Basil at around this time show a man without apparent eyesight problems and, throughout his life, he was physically fit enough to endure long hours of digging in the outdoors in all weathers.

Interestingly though, in his memoirs, Charles Phillips (who later took charge of the 1939 Sutton Hoo dig) records of Basil: "I would hazard a guess that he may have had a severe illness in his youth."[12] Eventually, on 16 October 1918, Basil Brown enrolled as a volunteer in the Suffolk Royal Army Medical Corps, serving for just over a year until the end of October 1919.[13]

It was soon after the war that Basil Brown met his future wife, Dorothy May Oldfield. May, as she was always known, was the daughter of a carpenter on the Wramplingham estate near Wymondham, and Basil and May had met in Cromer on the north Norfolk coast. She was nine years his junior. The couple were married in Rickinghall Superior Church on 27 June

May Brown – undated but probably 1920s (SCCAS)

1923 and afterwards settled into married life living and working with Basil's parents at Church Farm. They would have had little or no money of their own and what money they had was probably spent on books for Basil's studies.

Throughout their married life, the couple never owned a motor car although Basil held a driving licence for two years from June 1921; no competency tests were required at this time.[14] Instead, he cycled everywhere, near and far. From *Kelly's Directory* of 1925-26 we see that Basil has taken over the job of insurance agent from his father, George, and in August 1926 George Brown died at the age of sixty-three. He was buried in Rickinghall Superior churchyard where, four years later, his 73-year-old widow, Charlotte, was also buried.[15]

On the death of his father, Basil found himself taking on the tenancy of Church Farm. Arthur "Tinker" Francis who, as a boy, used to run errands for Rickinghall residents, recalled fetching milk from Church Farm. Basil kept a few cows, probably milking them himself but, according to Tinker, did little with the land which boasted more poppies than anything else! The Browns also kept a large billy goat which, on more than one occasion got out and into the nearby school playground.[16] So, by all accounts, Basil's heart was not in agriculture: when not trying to keep the farm afloat, his head was clearly buried in his books.

Looking to the stars
Basil had been accepted as a member of the British Astronomical Association in 1918, but his interest in heavenly bodies had started much earlier, as he recounts in one of his notebooks:

"My interest in astronomy dates I think from or near the year 1893, when I was five years old and what first aroused my interest in this sublime study, I do not remember. Having no scientific books at that time I used to make cuttings from our local paper, which used to publish science notes each week and paste them in a notebook being specifically attracted by the ones relating to astronomy... The first astronomical events I remember were very large meteors one of which was particularly notable as it appeared to be below the clouds in the evening, it was yellow in colour. The next event was an eclipse of the sun (partial). Having made various experiments with smoked glass at the time, my grandmother told me she remembered an eclipse of the sun (nearly total), years before the light effects of which during the eclipse, made all the linen on the clothes line look a dirty yellow colour."[17]

Basil also told a reporter from *The Daily Express*: "I was five when I started to take an interest in astronomy. My great-grandfather was interested in it, and I got hold of some of his old books and charts."[18]

Basil's contributions to meetings and the journal of the British Astronomical Association were numerous, especially his reports on various observations.[19] As far as it is known, Basil only ever owned one very modest telescope, so many of his observations were phenomena best seen with the naked eye, including the northern lights, meteors and comets. Reminiscing in later life about his astronomical observations, Basil wrote:

"In 1908 I met with a young fellow A E Hoskings who took an interest in astronomy. It is extremely rare in country districts that one finds someone who knows the stars. This gave me some encouragement and I bought a 2 in[ch] refractor which has given me great pleasure. This was in 1909. I have been able to observe three of four comets with my telescope, that of Halley in 1910 was a rather disappointing object in the telescope. Drake's Comet was a very obvious and good telescopic object. It was also very plainly visible to the naked eye. Moorhouse's was good. I have also observed some eclipses. One of the Sun was specially good, I saw both Mercury and Venus during the eclipse. This was the eclipse of Aug 21st 1914. I have been able since to observe many interesting things, including many observations of the Sun and Moon also of Saturn, Jupiter and Venus, the new star discovered by Miss Cook, Nova Aquilae, also many meteors which are recorded in my observing book."[20]

Basil had a particular interest in historical astronomical mapping and cataloguing, having two articles published in a popular, weekly science magazine, *The English Mechanic*.[21] He also wrote articles that were published in the *East Anglian Daily Times* such as his 1929 piece entitled "An Astronomical Riddle" in which he discusses whether the planet Mars might be inhabited. The following year, he wrote an article in the same paper about Pluto, the then newly discovered planet. It was no surprise, then, that Basil's only published book was a history of astronomical atlases, maps and charts.[22] It was written in his spare time in the space of four

Basil with his astronomical instruments – undated but probably 1930s (SCCAS)

Basil, May and Mr Armenter in front of Rickinghall School (SCCAS)

years.²³ It retailed at 18 shillings and received a reasonably favourable review in the *Journal of the British Astronomical Association*.

In the book, Basil thanks those who had assisted him in preparing his book for publication. The list is an impressive who's who of British astronomers and demonstrates the extent to which Basil depended on networking to supplement his own study. Indeed, his regular correspondents included those from overseas and one astronomer with whom he formed a friendship was a Mr Armenter from Spain. Armenter, together with his wife, visited the Browns during a trip to England. Basil Brown's aptitude for languages was highlighted in a feature on Basil in *The Daily Express* which tells us that he read and spoken Latin and French well, and that he also understood German and Spanish.²⁴ As with Basil's education in astronomy and archaeology, it is highly probable that the Harmsworth Self-Educator was his main textbook; it covered all these languages.

By the time of Mr and Mrs Armenter's visit to Rickinghall in May 1934, Basil and May Brown were living in the brick and flint house attached to Rickinghall School, where Basil had been educated. They were presumably renting it from the council during a period when it was not used to house the headteacher. Basil had finally decided to turn his back on agriculture: in the autumn of 1933, he had put all his farming stock up for sale and had vacated Church Farm.²⁵ Instead, to try to make ends meet, he offered his services as a handyman and odd-job man by day, digging gardens and cutting logs. By night, he studied his astronomy books, as well as all and everything he could lay his hands on relating to his other great passion of archaeology.

---

[1] Rickinghall National School logbook 1863-1880 (SA/B: ADB 540/1/1)
[2] The certificate is held by the SCCAS.
[3] Basil Brown Archive volume LVI (SA/I: Acc No 18855).
[4] This is held by the SCCAS.
[5] Accessed online at www.archive.org in April 2020.
[6] Basil Brown Archive volume XVII (SA/I: HD 3096/3/1) and Basil Brown Archive volume XVIII (SA/I: HD 3096/3/2).
[7] Basil Brown Archive volume LVII (SA/I: Acc No 18855).

[8] The SCCAS holds a copy of George Brown's employment contract with the Royal Insurance Company.
[9] *East Anglian Daily Times* 15 September 1908, page 3.
[10] *Diss Express* 5 November 1915, page 8.
[11] NT SH/BB2/PRIM/DOC/4a.
[12] Phillips, 1987.
[13] The SCCAS holds Basil's certificate of service in the Volunteer Force.
[14] The licence is now held by a private individual.
[15] The *Bury Free Press* of 11 September 1926, p 12 and the *Diss* Express 23 May 1930, p 4, respectively, carry reports of the funerals of George and Charlotte Brown.
[16] Tinker Francis was interviewed by Chris and Marcia Bell in 2004.
[17] Basil Brown Archive volume LVI (SA/I: HD 3096).
[18] *The Daily Express* 15 January 1935.
[19] A complete list of Basil's astronomical contributions is to be found in an online article by Bill Barton, FRAS, on www.oasi.org.uk.
[20] Basil Brown Archive volume LVI (SA/I: HD 3096).
[21] The two articles are "Star Atlases and Charts" in volume 119, issue 3071 of 1 February 1924 and "The Star Catalogues" in volume 120, issue 3105 of 26 September 1924.
[22] Brown, Basil, J W *Astronomical Atlases, Charts and Maps: An Historical and General Guide* (Search Publishing Co., London, 1932).
[23] "Basil Brown, Archaeologist" by Theodore Vincent Cutting in *East Anglian Magazine* volume 14, number 12 of October 1955.
[24] *The Daily Express* 15 January 1935.
[25] The *Diss Express* of 1 September 1933, page 1, carries an advertisement for the sale.

Chapter 3
First Archaeological Forays

*"If one takes the trouble to look carefully
he will notice indications of the past"*

As soon as Basil Brown decided to abandon farming in late 1933, he picked up a spade in earnest and embarked on his career as an archaeologist. When Basil and May left Church Farm, they needed to find somewhere to live. Their first move may well have been to a cottage in Rickinghall, but this location is now not known.[1] By May 1935 (and possibly earlier), however, the couple were living in the School House which was attached to Basil's former school in Hinderclay Road, Rickinghall.

Although this property was usually occupied by the headteacher, there was a short period that spring and summer when the school employed two temporary headmasters after the departure of F C Astle and before the arrival of F L G Reynolds. So, it is reasonable to assume that the Browns rented this vacant house for a short while before their move, in August 1935, to a rented property in Rickinghall in which they were to spend the rest of their lives. This was an end of terrace house called Cambria in The Street.[2]

The Browns were never very wealthy, and both worked hard to make ends meet. May Brown acted as local correspondent for several newspapers including the *Bury Free Press*, the *Diss Express* and the *East Anglian Daily Times*. She would report on church services, including weddings and funerals, as well as any other community events and news. May was a regular worshipper at church services whereas Basil reportedly was not.[3]

Basil did, however, take a keen interest in parish affairs. In May 1935, the Rickinghall Inferior Parish Council held a special meeting to discuss the severe shortage of housing, resulting in a motion to raise the matter urgently with the local authorities.[4] Basil, who at that time was seeking a permanent home in the village, questioned why neighbouring villages were benefitting from new-build council housing but Rickinghall Inferior was seemingly missing out.

Basil Brown Archive volume XCIII (SCCAS)

The Browns' house displayed a sign showing that they were insurance agents

Sometime later in life, Basil embarked on writing a book on archaeology, which he called *Suffolk Explorations.* This was to remain in manuscript form.[5] He opens with the following:

"If one takes the trouble to look carefully he will notice indications of the past which have been brought to the surface of fields by deep cultivation but there is a snag for incidentally these objects, tiles, pottery, glass, bronze objects which reach the surface in this way are intermixed with things of more recent times, and then one is faced with allocating each to its particular period but this becomes quite easy by practise. This knowledge has also to be supplemented by some geological lore and ability to recognise differences in soils and stones, all this is very helpful. Then again we have to consider the proximity of rivers, streams and springs, and what objects have been picked up or dug out by workers in the field and here the farmer may be useful for he or his workmen quite often have some interesting information to tell you, foundations may have been struck during ploughing, a drain may have been dug that has cut through an ancient cambered road where no road has been known, even in local tradition, and he may have a Roman coin found on the farm."

Throughout Basil's long archaeological career, he literally left no stone unturned in his quest to uncover the past, often persuading farmers and property owners to allow him to investigate what was beneath the surface.

A personal connection in Burgate

One of Basil's first archaeological forays was in the nearby parish of Burgate. This was at a property called Stubbing's Entry which held particular significance for Basil. It was where his paternal grandfather, John Brown, his wife and family had lived in the 1860s and 1870s and where Basil's father, George, had been born.[6] In a typescript note by Basil summarising his early motivations and explorations, he writes: "Interested in ancient alignments and studied borderline works (Astro-Archaeological) [such] as Lockyer's "Dawn of Astronomy", "Stonehenge" etc. Applied alignments by compass and measurements to sites of various moated sites and located the position of the buildings which had once existed by excavation in the enclosures in eight cases, and in one at Burgate a pavement of oyster shells cut and fitted together. All these were Medieval sites. Roman sites were unknown in this part of Suffolk and unsuspected."[7]

Even as a relatively inexperienced archaeologist, Basil was sufficiently confident and curious to take on an aspect on which little work had been done thus far. He was also not afraid to seek to have accounts of his research and excavations published. His early discoveries, however, at Burgate, Rickinghall (including live Roman snails[8]) and Hinderclay, were reported in the *Proceedings of the Suffolk Institute of Archaeology and Natural History* by Revd H A Harris rather than Basil himself: it is possible that this was merely because Basil was not yet a member of the institute.[9]

In August 1934, Basil received a rejection letter from the Eastern Daily Press to whom he had submitted an article (which may well have been on Stubbing's Entry). The short note states that the editor is unable to accept the article because: "He would rather wait until there has been an official excursion from either the Norfolk or Suffolk Archaeological Society."[10] At the *East Anglian Daily Times*, however, he had better luck. In 1936, having first submitted his article on Stubbing's Entry to the news editor, it was passed to the editor of "East Anglian Miscellany", a regular series of columns printed in the newspaper, resulting in the publication in two parts of Basil's account of his findings in Burgate.[11]

In his article Basil explains: "Extremely little of the ancient history of many moated enclosures in Suffolk is known but this applies to large numbers of Medieval sites scattered throughout the land. So sometime ago I attempted a few researches into the past as contained in records etc and also through the courtesy of Mr Curry the owner and occupier of the farm, I was enabled to make a few excavations within the larger moated enclosure, where once had undoubtedly stood a large house of manorial type." He then summarises his findings from his research into deeds and charters dating back to the thirteenth century, as well as detailing his main archaeological discovery at the site, which was a pavement of oyster shells: "Hundreds of shells were found, laid and fitted together, at a depth of 13 inches, and covering an area of several feet." An entry in one of Basil's notebooks dated 17 April 1934 expands on this, stating that the pavement was 30 by 20 feet "(deduced)" adding that: "Excavations made but had to cover up shells owing to the poultry."[12]

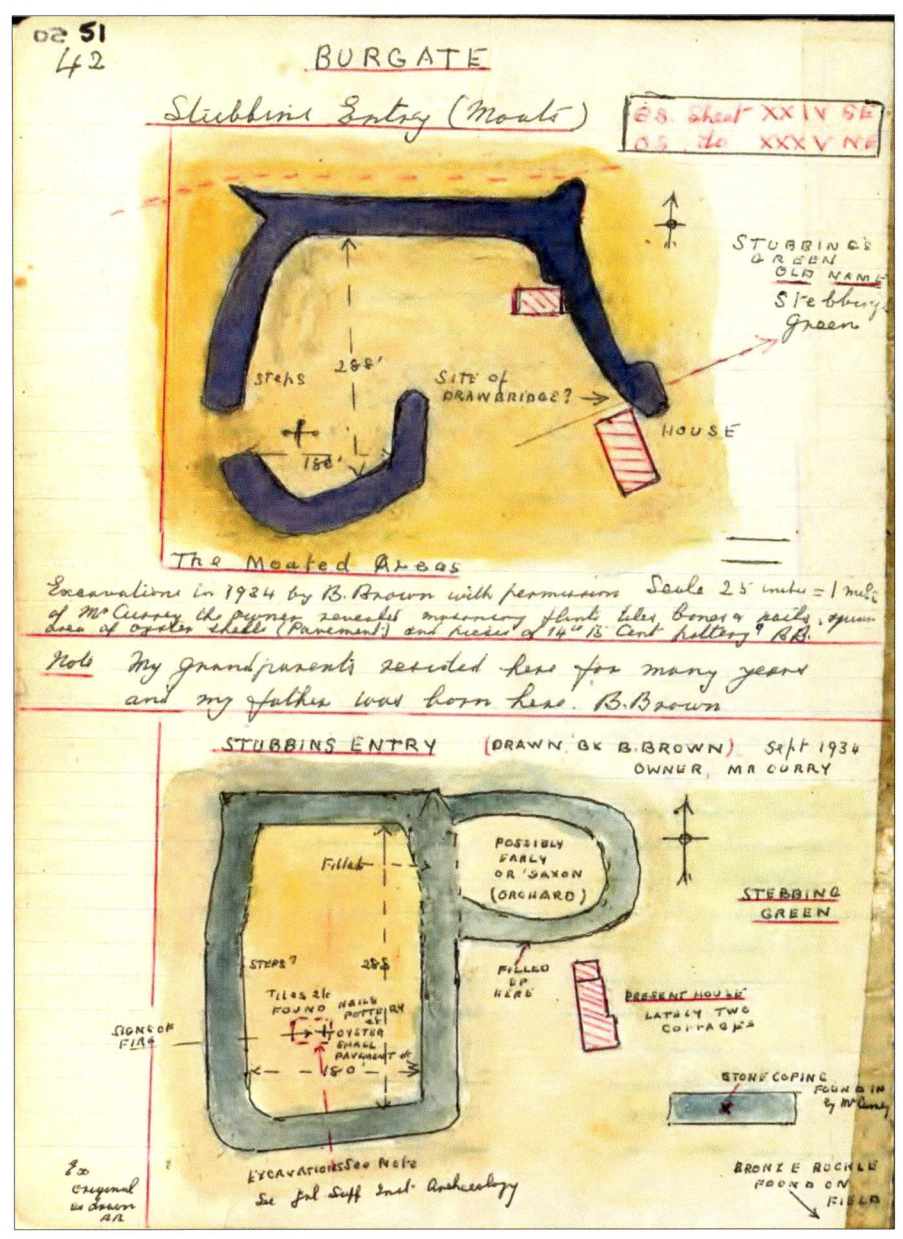

A page from Basil Brown Archive volume XX (SCCAS)

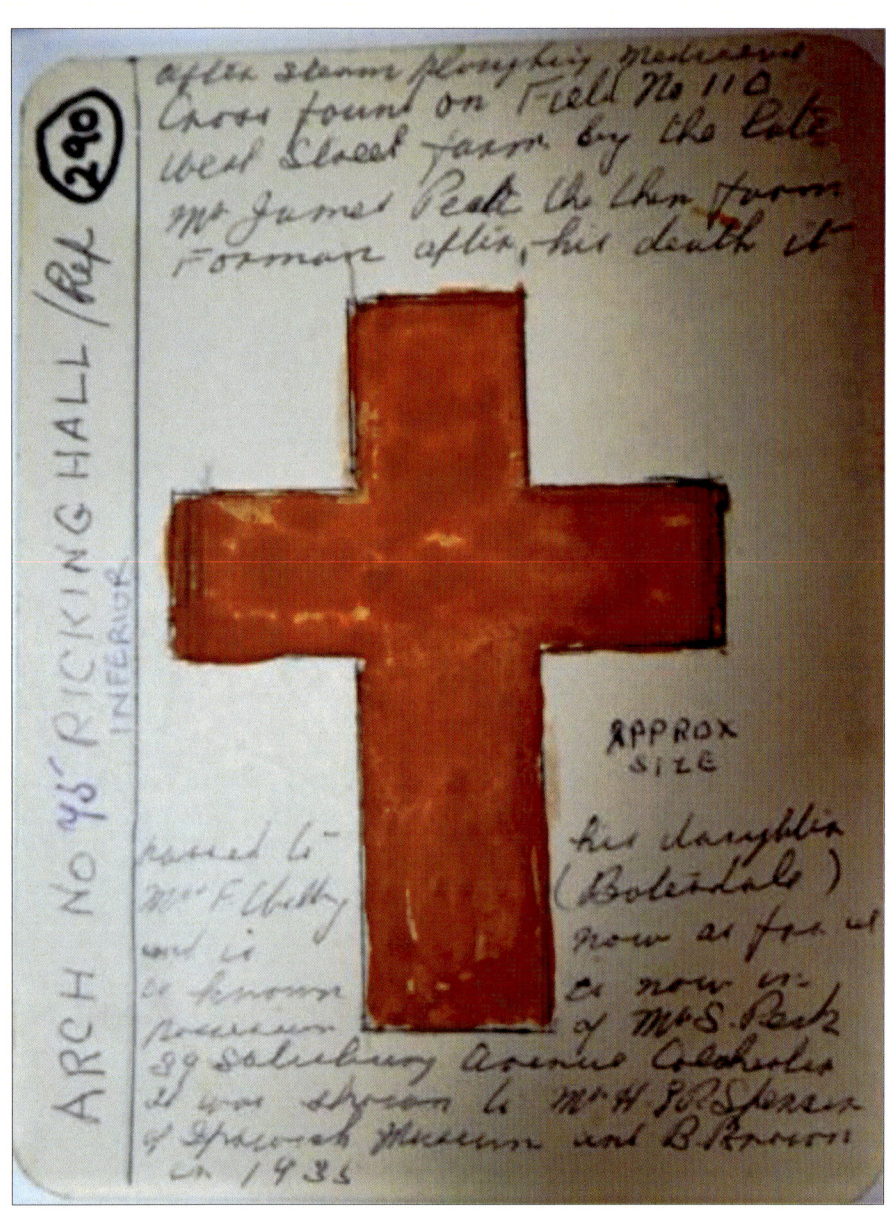

From Basil Brown Card Index No. 1 (SCCAS)

On the trail of knights

A series of his notebooks dating from the mid-1930s reveals how a single find prompted Basil to devote a considerable amount of time and energy to researching local links to Knights Templar and Knights Hospitaller (known in full as the Order of Knights of the Hospital of Saint John of Jerusalem).[13] Basil records that a medieval red glass or crystal cross was found on a large field to the north of West Street Farm in around 1900. It was uncovered during steam ploughing by the farm's foreman, James Pesk, and his son and daughter had shown the cross to Harold Spencer from Ipswich Museum and Basil Brown in February 1935. The seeming significance of this find was that it was 1½ miles from a field named Temple Close on old maps.[14]

Basil's meticulous and lengthy historical notes cover manors, and other known medieval sites in Suffolk (and even further afield), known or thought to relate to these ancient military orders. Naturally, he concentrates on those closer to home such as those in Rickinghall, Botesdale, Redgrave, Burgate, Mellis and Gislingham, in particular. He notes that Rickinghall's Temple Close was, at one time, copyhold land of the manor of Mellis St John's and that there are various documentary references to a Preceptory of Knights Templars in Gislingham.[15] In October 1934, the Rector of Gislingham appealed for information from local residents on the probable site of a "monastery" in the parish. He explains that tradition had it that there was once a building in Rush Green Field opposite the entrance to the Rectory drive, where Basil had uncovered rubble foundations. He notes that: "During this year and subsequently till the outbreak of the war in 1939 we endeavoured to locate the site."[16]

The archaeological "go-to" man

Basil soon established himself as the local "go-to" man for all things archaeological and historical. One of Basil's notebooks dating from this time shows that he was collating information about any intriguing local finds.[17] Most of the entries are brief and many note that these are "not yet investigated" or similar wording, implying that he intended to follow up on these at a later date." In Botesdale, Basil notes that: "In Mr Last's butcher's yard is a curious ancient stone which may have been a portion of market cross. Ap 20th 1934." and at Uplands in Rickinghall: "In garden I made a small excavation and located masonry at depth of 3½ Ft. Mr R.W. Whitmore, M.A., owner tells me it extends 30 yards. away in paddock. This probably an ancient road or trackway. Probably the Romans occupied the hill. Ap 17th 1934."

One of Basil's other notes in this book relates to Money Pot Farm in Redgrave. He records that a Roman urn was found which was reportedly in Moyses Hall Museum in Bury St Edmunds. He says: "I visited this site with the Rev. Percy Robinson and could, in a small triangular plantation, locate a hard surface at 2ft 6in. May be a layer of small stones (not further investigated Ap 17th 1934)." Basil also recorded another find at Money Pot Hill which had been discovered by Mr Gilbey in 1929. This coin had reportedly been taken to the British Museum in 1930 who had identified it as one dating from the reign of the Roman Emperor, Nero.[18] Despite these tantalising clues to Roman occupation, this is one site to which Basil apparently never returned to undertake further investigation.

In Jacobites Wood, a long, wooded stretch with Botesdale Lodge near its southern tip, Basil reports that a green glazed brick was found ("now in the possession of Mr F Cannell, Botesdale"). He further notes that this was the site of tile kilns which were worked in the Stuart and later period and that: "some trials by B Brown and F Cannell, Botesdale".[19] In Rickinghall, too, some glazed pottery was uncovered by Basil himself. This was on land occupied by a then new-build and he recorded the find in 1934 as late Tudor. He later elaborated on this, also amending his initial thoughts about the dating of the pottery, recording: "Gardenhouse Lane opposite the Gardenhouse once an inn on the east side of lane a bungalow has been built and early glazed sherds were found, the glaze varies from apple green, dark green and orange and appears to be 13th-14th century. The fields were known as Howchin's Close from a family of that name who resided near. This way which once connected Temple Lane, Manor Farm, Gislingham in medieval times has various sites Bronze Age, Roman and Saxon along its route."[20]

A window "burglariously" entered

As the oldest surviving structure in the neighbourhood, it is not surprising that Basil returned to the round-towered church of Rickinghall Inferior at various times during his life in the village. It certainly appears that from the outset, Basil ensured he was at the very centre of any investigation into the unknown. A press cutting from the *Suffolk Chronicle and Mercury* from 16

August 1935 in one of his notebooks reveals how he "aided and abetted" Revd H A Harris in a foray into the first-floor room of the porch of the church.[21] Revd Harris' article entitled "Rickinghall St Mary Church Porch: An archaeological exploration" explains that following a visit by members of the Suffolk Institute of Archaeology, their curiosity was aroused by a room over the church porch but which had no reasonable means of entrance apart from a grated window to the front, over the door.

So, returning to investigate, Harris writes: "The Rector having given me permission to explore this mysterious apartment, I borrowed a ladder from Miss Tuck, and with the help of Mr Basil Browne *[sic]*, burglariously removed the iron bars of the grated window and squeezed through into a compartment, the floor of which was well nigh kneedeep with the accumulated dust of ages and the debris left by generations of nesting birds, together with stones thrown in by those who had made the window their target." He continues by recording their finds in the small chamber which included an old hassock (kneeler) and a rather dilapidated, empty wooden chest (which Harris noted was probably once the parish chest where important documents and registers were kept). The mystery of a room without an entrance was solved, however, since from the inside a doorway and flight of stairs was found which led down to a point in the extreme south-west of the nave which had since been plastered over.

On the trail of the Romans
Basil developed a passion for the Roman period at an early age, and many of his early archaeological forays were in search of evidence of Roman occupation in East Anglia. At that time, such evidence was patchy. Basil was a member of the Roman Roads Society, and his notebooks demonstrate that he was keen to develop a sounder understanding of where such roads in the region had been built, especially when they crossed his own neighbourhood.

At an early stage, he was pointed towards Hamblyn House which sits on the parish borders of Rickinghall Superior and Botesdale. Nowadays it is an English Heritage Grade II* listed property which, has in its long history, served as a mill owner's house, as well as a country club. In 1934, Basil writes: "In the garden were found many pottery fragments and bones, apparently Roman. Excavations made, bones and oyster shells found (no

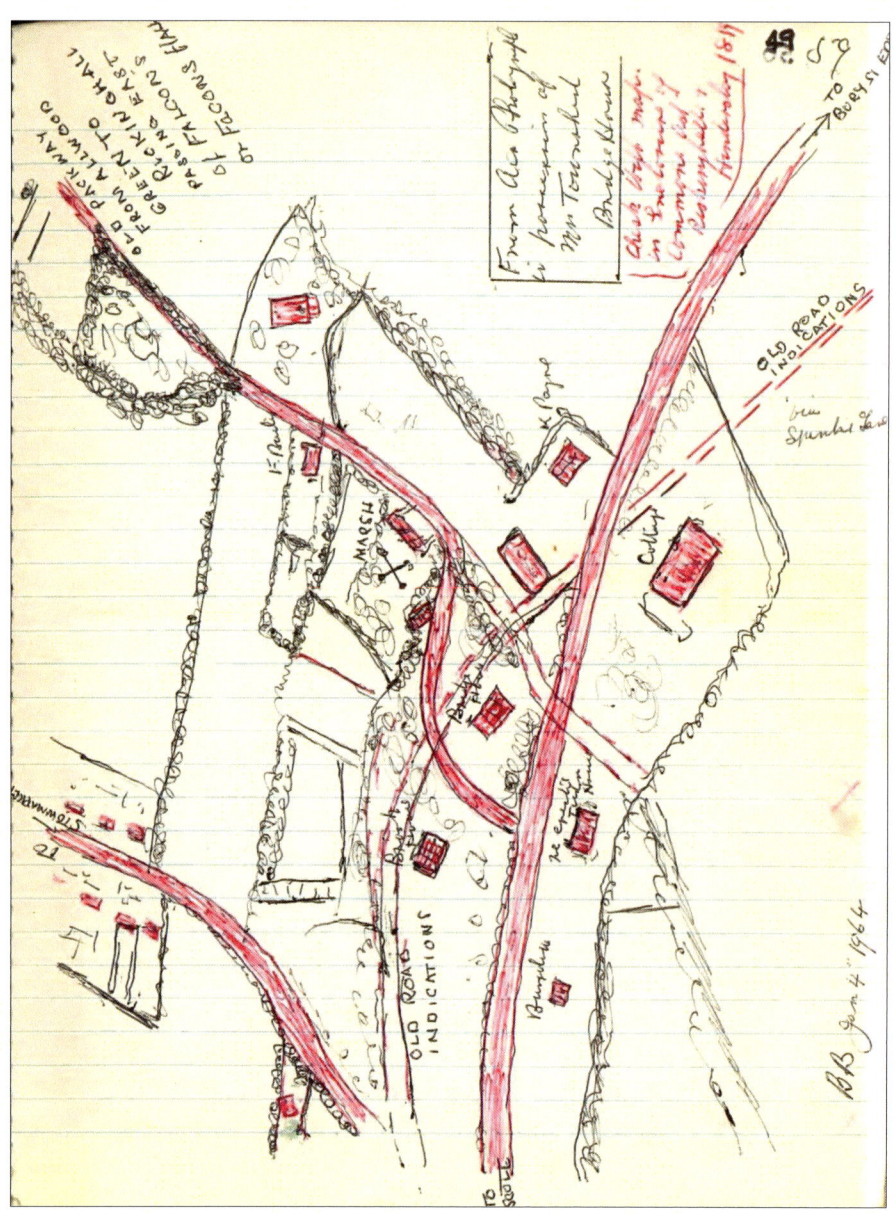

A page from Basil Brown Archive volume XIII with Basil's sketch of Roman Roads (SCCAS)

masonry)." A further notebook reveals that he also found small pieces of charcoal and that "there is a hard stratum of small stones on the hill slope" and even later he records that the garden of Hamblyn House lies on the line of a track from a Roman burial or cemetery running north, noting that when gas pipes were being laid nearby in the mid-nineteenth century, some fifteen small, Roman glass bottles were unearthed. This was a site which Basil returned to when an opportunity arose and in November 1943, he was able to examine the suspected Roman track, writing: "Excavations for cable laying revealed evidence of good cambered road approx. 16 ft. wide."[22]

Basil spent some time researching earlier courses of the roads in Rickinghall and one to which he returned at various times was at the west end of the village. He notes that the Inferior Church sat almost on the line of a Roman Road. A photograph in one of his notebooks shows the present course of the stream running alongside the south side of the churchyard which he notes was diverted in around 1790. A second photo is taken from his former school and is captioned: "Ancient course of stream on this side of church."[23]

Further afield
Basil Brown's early archaeological curiosity was not just confined to Rickinghall and the surrounding area. In 1935, he wrote a letter requesting permission to dig on the Elveden Hall estate, then owned by Lord Iveagh. Basil had reason to believe that evidence of a Roman settlement might be found there, but his application was turned down on the basis that another party was already engaged in a similar investigation. The reply from the estate office suggested that Basil might reapply in a year's time with an accompanying map showing the exact site of a proposed dig.[24] It appears that Basil did not pursue this avenue again: he had, instead, found a larger project nearer to home.

---

[1] Local historians were once told that Basil had lived at a cottage now called Baylees in The Street (but at an earlier date of 1912), not far from Church Farm, but we have not been able to verify this.
[2] We are able to pin down Basil's moves to the School House and to Cambria from surviving letters sent to him at these addresses.

[3] Interestingly, though, a report in the *Bury Free Press* of 3 April 1937 of the Vestry Meeting at Rickinghall, records that Basil did not seek re-election onto the Parochial Church Council, implying that he had previously served on the council.

[4] The *Bury Free Press* of 25 May 1935, p 4, carries a report of the meeting.

[5] *Suffolk Explorations* is an unfinished (or partly lost) typescript manuscript written by Basil Brown and now held by the SSCAS.

[6] The family appear here in the 1861 census return (TNA: RG09/1149/20/1) and the 1871 census return (TNA: RG10/1736/21/1).

[7] A typescript note by Basil held by SCCAS.

[8] *Helix pomatia* – descendants of edible snails originally brought to Britain by the Romans.

[9] *Proceedings of the Suffolk Institute of Archaeology and Natural History* Vol XXI, Part 3 (1933), page 263.

[10] The original letter is held by the SCCAS in Basil Brown Archive volume LXXXXVII.

[11] The original letter is held by the SCCAS in Basil Brown Archive volume LXXXXVII. Cuttings from the *East Anglian Daily Times* of this article are pasted into Basil Brown Archive volume XXII (SA/I: Acc No 18855).

[12] Basil Brown Archive volume XCIV (SA/I: HD 3096/1/3).

[13] Basil Brown Archive volumes XX, XXI and XXII (SA/I: Acc No 18855).

[14] The enclosure map for Rickinghall Superior dated 1819 shows two adjacent fields called Temple Close and Temple Field (SA/I: B150/1/2.4).

[15] The Knights Hospitaller took over the Gislingham estate when the Knights Templars were disbanded in 1311.

[16] A cutting from the *Hartismere Deanery Magazine* with the clergyman's appeal for information is pasted into Basil Brown Archive volume XXII (SA/I: Acc No 18855). This is followed by Basil's copious notes on his explorations and research.

[17] Basil Brown Archive volume XCIV (SA/I: HD 3096/1/3).

[18] Basil Brown Archive volume XCIV (SA/I: HD 3096/1/3), Basil Brown Archive volume XXXVII (SA/I: Acc No 18855) and Basil Brown Archive Card Index No. 1 (SA/I: Acc No 18855).

[19] Basil Brown Archive volume XCIV (SA/I: HD 3096/1/3) and Basil Brown Archive Card Index No. 1 (SA/I: Acc No 18855).

[20] Basil Brown Archive volume XCIV (SA/I: HD 3096/1/3) and Basil Brown Archive Card Index No. 1 (SA/I: Acc No 18855).

[21] Basil Brown Archive volume XXIII (SA/I: Acc No 18855).

[22] These various entries are to be found in Basil Brown Archive volume XXXI (SA/I: Acc No 18855), Basil Brown Archive volume XCIII (SA/I: HD 3096/1/5) and Basil Brown Archive volume XCVII (SA/I: HD 3096/2/2).

[23] Basil Brown Archive volume XCIII (SA/I: HD 3096/1/5).

[24] The original letter can be found in Basil Brown Archive volume XCIV (SA/I: HD 3096/1/3).

Chapter 4
Employment

"Basil Brown, Archaeologist"

Cork Wood

It was in 1934 that Basil first turned his attention to a wood in Rickinghall which bordered an area called Foxledge Common in the parish of Wattisfield. He writes:

> "Fragments of Roman pottery had been found by me in Hamlyn [sic] House garden in Rickinghall [which] aroused my curiosity and I made inquiries regarding similar pottery found in the vicinity as a natural supposition would be that somewhere round about there had been Roman habitations and my notebook records that fragments of similar pottery had been found in Calke Wood (earlier called Cork Wood) led to a visit to the wood and making enquiries of Messrs Henry Watson & Sons owners of the present pottery at Wattisfield who obtain their clay from pits in the wood and from some of their employees all were very helpful and I at once proceeded to explore the wood and the nearby fields. A little later April 17th 1934 I noticed many fragments of Roman pottery strewn about a field on the opposite or Wattisfield side of Calke Wood Road, and here I reached a dead end for trials made on the field in the wood yielded little. "[1]

Basil's suspicions that this was the site of Roman pottery works were, however, so strong that he was not to be deterred so easily. Also, workers at Watson's pottery works, whose interest had been aroused by the earlier finds, kept a look out for similar fragments which yielded a spectacular result in July 1934 of an almost complete Roman urn near where the first trial excavations had been carried out.[2] It was at this early stage that Mr J B Watson began to take a close interest in Basil's explorations and started helping Basil with field research and weekend excavations. They formed a close friendship. Others assisted Basil, including Mr Black, the owner of Walnut Tree Farm in Wattisfield, and his foreman, Mr Miller. Mr F Mole, the owner of Calke Wood also lent an enthusiastic hand.

The first kiln is discovered
It was on Christmas Day in 1934 that Basil made a breakthrough. This may be surprising even to many hard-working modern-day archaeologists. However, for Basil, every waking moment was spent in his quest to unearth the history beneath his feet. He records:
"Some nicely worked Neolithic flints turned up but no satisfactory signs that the scent was hot and as time was getting on we left off digging and walked across the field opposite and then I noticed some small fragments of pottery close together in association with stones coloured red & blue. A trial hole revealed the characteristic sooty black earth and large pieces of Roman pottery."
The first kiln was located the following day – Boxing Day.

The *Diss Express* of 11 January 1935 reported on these early finds of Basil's: "Mr J Watson (Ipswich) and Mr Basil Brown of Rickinghall have made interesting archaeological discoveries at Foxledge. These are the remains of a Roman pottery kiln and well unearthed in a field near the Wattisfield-Rickinghall parish boundary, adjoining Cork Wood, where a Roman urn was dug out in July. Very few Roman potteries are recorded in Suffolk, which makes the present find of great interest." And in the *Proceedings of the Suffolk Institute of Archaeology and Natural History*, Basil himself expands on what was discovered at this first kiln site:
"The ground was found to contain many irregular tabular fragments of hard baked clay, black, brown, and red in colour and bearing on both sides the imprint of straw, hay, twigs and possibly reeds and rushes. Apparently these were the debris from the top or dome of the kiln which would require reconstruction after each firing. Subsequent excavation suggested that a layer of rough gravel and sand surrounding this kiln was continued between it and the neighbouring kilns, thus forming tracks alongside which had been dug a shallow trench or ditch, found to contain residue from the kilns and other debris, consisting of sooty black earth, charcoal, stones which had been subjected to heat, and animal bones, principally those of oxen and pigs. Very few oyster shells were seen. The rest of the dumped material consisted of broken pottery and the before-mentioned pieces of burnt clay from the kiln top. Near the site of the kiln itself were the remains of dumps of mixed clay."[3]

Basil working on a Bronze Age shaft in Calke Wood – undated but probably 1930s

One expert who co-wrote the *Proceedings* article was Revd Ivan E Moore, a specialist on the Roman era. He later wrote: "The first time I saw Basil Brown was on a damp and dingy day in early January 1935. He was standing in a hole with a spade in his hand and heaps of earth all around him, before him his find, the Roman pottery kiln. Whenever I saw him down the years that is how I always found him on site, that was his metier, digging."[4]

More Roman pottery kilns

Basil later wrote of how six kilns were uncovered in quick succession:
 "Next day came the discovery of the first Wattisfield pot kiln. This was followed by a second and a third kiln about equidistant either side of the first. All three kilns had been smashed but it was possible to define both shapes and position of the furnaces from the brilliant red clay. The field was then ploughed and in doing this indications of a fourth kiln were found, this I examined and recorded. Subsequent explorations revealed sites five and six with similar evidence. Specimens were taken of pottery at each and sites covered down."

By now, Basil had a better understanding of the layout of the Roman pottery kilns. He records:
 "It was now evident from the relative positions of these six kiln sites that the kiln sites had been arranged to a definite plan, which appeared to be a large rectangular enclosure kilns forming the line of this enclosure, the interior being taken up with clay pits and probably some timber built sheds. Through the centre ran a raised track, while the potters huts seem to have been outside the enclosure to the west. After allowing for a second track leading towards what is now Cork Wood taking place of a kiln I measured the spacing distance (i.e. 72 feet on either side) which brought me into the strip of grass land, and there moles had brought up black earth. All that had to be done was to pick the spot undisturbed by moles but surrounded by mole hills and put down a trial hole which came in the exact centre of the stand of kiln No. 7."
A further four pottery kilns were revealed shortly afterwards.

An Anglo-Saxon burial

Basil noted that four human skeletons had reportedly been found, around 68 years before his excavations at Wattisfield, in a chalk pit.[5] At 4pm on

Monday 3 February 1936, he recorded: "Further evidence of burials on ridge discovered today by B. Brown. When three trial holes were put down on ridge situated between Cork Wood and the farm buildings (Walnut Tree Farm), the 3rd trial bringing to light human bones, iron knife and an unknown iron object."[6] Later, Basil concluded that this site had probably been an Anglo-Saxon cemetery and, as well as the iron knife he had found, he believed that the men may also have been buried with shields which had perished in the chalk over the centuries.[7] The skeleton and iron objects were removed and taken to the Ipswich Museum.

Ipswich Museum

It was the discovery of the Wattisfield kilns which proved a pivotal moment in Basil Brown's archaeological career. Basil had reported the discovery of kiln 7, in February 1935, to his friend Revd Harris who, in turn, informed Guy Maynard, the Curator of the Ipswich Museum. The kiln was subsequently completely excavated, removed and installed in the museum alongside specimens of pottery found at the site. Following his appointment in 1920, Maynard, together with James Reid Moir, the museum's President, had developed the archaeological work of the institution. Reports of archaeological finds at various of the museum's excavations across Suffolk were published by the Suffolk Institute of Archaeology and Natural History.

So, Basil came to the attention of Guy Maynard just at a time when the curator was looking to further expand archaeological excavation in the county. Having proved his credentials by uncovering these Roman pottery kilns, as well as in need of a regular income, Basil was employed by the Ipswich Museum as an archaeological excavator.

Basil, a largely self-educated working-class 47-year-old man, was at last following his boyhood dream of digging up history for a living. He had, however, no formal qualifications in archaeology. So, although his job title was that of archaeological excavator working under a qualified professional, we can forgive Basil's enthusiasm for his new role. At some stage he had an ink stamp made bearing the words "Basil Brown, Rickinghall Diss, Archaeologist."[8]

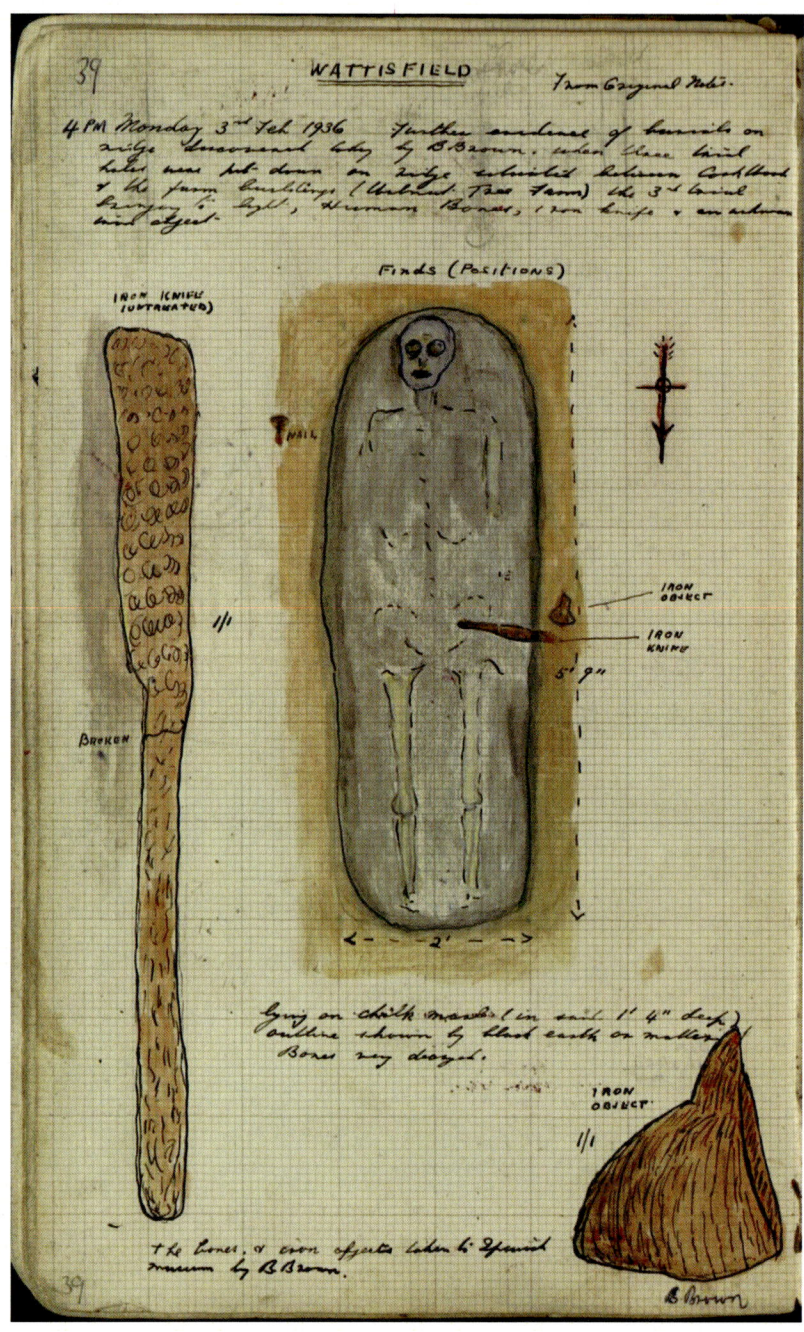

A page from Basil Brown Archive volume XCI (SCCAS)

Basil Brown: Archaeological Excavator

Basil's first two excavations for the Ipswich Museum were on Stuston Common and at Scole, which both lie on the Suffolk/Norfolk border. The Suffolk Institute of Archaeology and Natural History also had a stake in the digs, and articles in the institute's *Proceedings* detail how the work undertaken by Brown and C H Gale confirmed that Scole had been an important Roman settlement, sitting at the crossroads of two main Roman roads traversing the region.[9] Indeed, the *Diss Express* of 10 April 1936 reported that: "Further excavations made during last week on the site of the Roman encampment at Stuston Common have revealed evidence that the camp extended both sides of the River Waveney." Evidence unearthed by Basil and his fellow archaeologist included large pieces of Roman urns, bowls, dishes and other utensils. The figure of a Roman slave appeared on one piece of pottery. Foundations of Roman buildings were also excavated, including a sizeable villa which had been destroyed by fire.

The same newspaper, just over a month later, on 15 May, revealed that Basil and Mr Gale had established from their latest finds that the Roman settlement had been occupied during at least two separate periods. Two different types of floor, one of flints and the other of a kind of mortar, had been uncovered. A coin dating from between 117 and 138 AD had been found, as well as the base of a Samian ware pottery vessel which could be dated to between 68 and 98 AD.

Romans in Rickinghall

One of Basil's early local archaeological investigations had been in fields adjoining Gardenhouse Lane in Rickinghall. As and when he could, Basil returned to this site, having persuaded the landowners to allow him to dig, when the fields were not being cultivated. As the *Diss Express* reported: "Fragments of Roman pottery were first noticed on Mr Perry's field by Mr Basil Brown, of Rickinghall, in 1935 … The recent explorations on the sites near Gardenhouse Lane have resulted in various objects of interest being dug up from an extensive Romano-British occupation layer, about two feet below the present ground surface." The article reports of the find of a Roman coin of Delmatius in near mint condition and concludes: "By proving that a Romano-British settlement definitely existed at Rickinghall, along the probable road line from the coast inland puts our knowledge of the

Romanised communities of our district and incidentally throws further light upon the connections between them, in the far off past."[10]

Basil was to return many times to his home village and the adjacent parishes to excavate in search of further signs of Roman occupation. First, though, Guy Maynard tasked him with a larger-scale excavation in Stanton, some six miles west of Rickinghall.

Stanton Chare
Basil's excavations at Stanton Chare began on 5 October 1935 and, over the course of the next three years, he undertook four separate phases of excavation.[11] The winter months were naturally avoided. Throughout the project, Basil submitted weekly, typed reports to the Ipswich Museum. His daily excavation diary survives which covers the first phase of the dig, as well as a diary starting on 3 May 1937 (the beginning of the third phase).[12] The dig yielded some spectacular results, namely remains of a large Roman villa complex. This included two groups of bath buildings. Finds included over 100 coins dating from the 1st to the 4th century, a large collection of pottery (some bearing the potter's stamps) and many personal items such as bracelets, rings and brooches. Building material uncovered included multi-coloured, painted wall plaster, roof tiles and tesserae (mosaic tiles).

It is Basil that can take the credit for such a significant find as this in Suffolk. As Basil, himself, recorded some time after the dig:
"This important Roman settlement has deservedly received a good deal of attention and some thousands of visitors from all parts of the country and overseas have been to the site since the excavations have been proceeding. And the Press has published paragraphs describing the remains of the Roman buildings which have been cleared and the variety of interesting objects which have been dug out such as pottery, coins, ornaments etc. which were used by the inhabitants in the days when Britain was a province of Rome. As the find of this Roman settlement was due to field archaeology and the question which nearly every visitor asks is 'How was this found[?]'."[13]

He continues by explaining that having located a substantial pottery-making centre in Wattisfield but no evidence of any significant buildings, Basil believed that a large Roman villa must have existed in the vicinity. He therefore looked at the possible path of Roman roads together with records

Stanton Chare Roman villa excavation (Courtesy of Peter Christie)

of historic finds from the same period. After this paragraph, however, this is sadly where Basil's account (and his whole *Suffolk Explorations* manuscript) ends. So, we shall never read the answer solely in his own words. Instead, though, an article co-authored by Maynard and Brown explains the background.[14] In it, we learn that Basil had found fragments of Roman tiles and pottery in a field adjoining Stanton Chare Farm and sought information on any possible building foundations the farmers might have unearthed in the past.[15] In the summer of 1935, therefore, Basil returned to the site and dug some trial trenches together with J B Watson and Major Gilbert Kilner (of the Ixworth Cyder Factory). Some painted wall plaster was found which provided evidence of a high-quality residence.

Museum in a Barley Field

"Good use is being made of the opportunities for popular education offered by the excavation of the ruins of the Roman buildings recently discovered at Stanton Chair, near Ixworth. Many of the inhabitants of the neighbouring villages and others from greater distances have visited the site, particularly on Sunday afternoons and evenings, when parties are conducted round the excavations, and short talks given by those in charge on the Roman civilisation in Britain and the significance of the remains now exposed."

So starts an article in the *Bury Free Press* with the subtitle "A Museum in a Barley Field".[16] It tells readers that a temporary museum had also been set up at Stanton to showcase the finds. Visitors could also look at illustrations showing a reconstruction of the Roman villa.

Many interested societies organised visits to the Stanton Chare dig site, including the Ipswich Natural History Society together with members from the Suffolk Institute of Archaeology and Natural History. An article reporting on this excursion reports that Guy Maynard, who addressed the group: "… explained that the discovery was due to the enthusiasm and acute sense of field archaeology of Mr Basil Brown …"[17] Maynard clearly respected Basil's skills and was ready to give credit where it was due.

Helpers welcome

We can see from Basil's notes that even with his very early digs, he always welcomed helpers, both young and old, to join him. When the Stanton excavation resumed in May 1937, the local paper not only carried a short piece about the opportunities to visit the site, but it also encouraged volunteer workers to come forward.[18] Interestingly, there is a two-page table of dates and names in the back of one of Basil's Stanton excavation notebooks which may be a record of helpers on the dig.[19]

Honorary Member

The Stanton Chare excavation project, led by the Ipswich Museum, was funded partly by the Suffolk Institute of Archaeology and Natural History. The institute's grant was for £25, which went some way to covering Basil's agreed salary of £2 per week. In January 1937, Basil received the welcome news that the institute's Council had elected him an honorary member, allowing Basil to benefit from all membership privileges of subscribing members, but without having to pay an annual subscription.[20] As well as no doubt being welcome news financially, it was an honour of which Basil was no doubt justly proud after such a short period working in the field.

The fourth and final excavation phase at Stanton Chare started on 26 March 1938 and continued until 3 December of the same year. Basil was, however, not on site for seven weeks over the summer. Instead, he was digging elsewhere in Suffolk, at Sutton Hoo.

---

[1] This piece and subsequent quotes in this chapter about Calke Wood are taken from *Suffolk Explorations*, an unfinished (or partly lost) typescript manuscript written by Basil Brown and now held by the SSCAS.

[2] A comprehensive article on the pottery-making site at Foxledge Common, with contributions by Guy Maynard, Basil Brown, W G Grimes and Ivan Moore was published in *Proceedings of the Suffolk Institute of Archaeology and Natural History* Vol XXII, Part 2 (1935), pages 178-197.

[3] Ibid.

[4] Revd Moore's memoirs are held by his family.

[5] *Proceedings of the Suffolk Institute of Archaeology and Natural History* Vol XXII, Part 2 (1935), pages 178-197.

[6] Basil Brown Archive volume XCI (SA/I: HD 3096/1/4).

[7] Basil Brown Archive Card Index No. 1 (SA/I: Acc No 18855).

[8] This appears stamped in the front of Basil Brown Archive volume XCI (SA/I: HD 3096/1/4).

[9] *Proceedings of the Suffolk Institute of Archaeology and Natural History* Vol XXII, Part 3 (1936), pages 263-286.

[10] *Diss Express* 26 February 1937, page 7.
[11] The modern-day spelling of the place is "Chair", but Basil used the historical spelling.
[12] These records appear in Basil Brown Archive volume LXIII (SA/I: Acc No 18855), Basil Brown Archive volume XLVIII (SA/I: Acc No 18855) and Basil Brown Archive volume XLVI (SA/I: Acc No 18855) respectively.
[13] *Suffolk Explorations*, an unfinished (or partly lost) typescript manuscript written by Basil Brown, now held by the SSCAS.
[14] G Maynard and B Brown, 'The Roman Settlement at Stanton Chair (Chare) near Ixworth, Suffolk', *Proceedings of the Suffolk Institute of Archaeology and Natural History* Vol XXII, Part 3 (1936), Pages 339-341.
[15] The *Proceedings* article states that Basil's first field walking finds were in the autumn of 1933, although Basil's *Suffolk Explorations* says this was in November 1934.
[16] *Bury Free Press* 5 September 1936. page 8.
[17] *Bury Free Press* 26 September 1936. page 16.
[18] *Diss Express* 21 May 1937, page 9.
[19] Basil Brown Archive volume XLVI (SA/I: Acc No 18855).
[20] Basil received a personal letter from Revd Harris tipping him off about the election. The original letter is held by the SCCAS in Basil Brown Archive volume LXXXVIII. He also received official notification from the Honorary Financial Secretary. Basil kept this letter in his treasured collection of personal papers, now held by the SCCAS.

Chapter 5
The Sutton Hoo Years

"I am leaving nothing to chance, as the small things often count"

A first sight of Sutton Hoo

Basil Brown arrived at Sutton Hoo for the first time on Monday 20 June 1938. He had negotiated the terms of his employment the previous Friday with Guy Maynard, the curator of the Ipswich Museum. Basil was to be employed for the duration of his stay by the owner of the Sutton Hoo estate, Mrs Edith Pretty, at a rate of 30 shillings a week plus free accommodation (with Mrs Pretty's chauffeur, Bill Lyons, at White Cottage in the nearby village of Bromeswell), during which time he was to investigate a group of mounds on her land. Guy Maynard had viewed the mounds at Sutton Hoo the previous year after Mrs Pretty had asked the historian Vincent Redstone for advice on a possible excavation. Over the weekend, Basil had collected together some relevant literature based on information from Maynard and therefore went armed with excavation reports and other papers on the Bronze Age, early Iron Age, Roman and Anglo-Saxon periods.

Basil's diary entry for the day of his arrival is lengthy as he records every decision made that day.[1] After meeting Edith Pretty, he writes: "Mrs Pretty then took me to see the mounds, which were much hidden by bracken, and was rather alarmed by their sizes which were I found on examination far larger than Mr Maynard had led me to expect." Basil also records that Mrs Pretty had, at first, suggested that he might start excavation of the largest mound (called Tumulus I by Basil and subsequently numbered Mound 1). However, Basil had noticed signs of disturbance to the western side of the mound and a brief investigation revealed nothing of significance. Two labourers on the Sutton Hoo estate, Bert Fuller and Tom Sawyer, had been detailed by their employer to help Basil and so the trio began excavation of the circular Mound 3 (Basil's Tumulus A), which showed little disturbance other than by rabbits, the following day.

The first ship burial

On Wednesday 22 June, Basil records in his diary: "It should be noted that the exploration should be quick, i.e. to take about a fortnight, the idea being to prove if the mounds did or did not contain any remains ... Carried on with the trench carefully examining soils, in fact anything which can be regarded as possible clues. I am leaving nothing to chance, as the small things often count." Barely a week later, small fragments of bones and some sort of wood were found. On Friday 1 July, Basil writes: "The looked-for result at last, wood was found but not cleared. It may be a box or part of a boat." The following day, he records that several small fragments of objects were excavated including "a sherd of Anglo-Saxon pottery (part of a burial urn) ... a mass of corroded iron (afterwards found to be a battle axe)." and he states: "It is probable that grave robbers had disturbed this burial very soon after it took place and any valuable objects removed."

The first rivet
On Wednesday 6 July, after Basil had taken a short break back in Rickinghall, he and his helpers embarked on an excavation of a further, larger barrow (Basil's Tumulus D and later Mound 2). As with Mound 3, a trench was chosen to run east-west, which also aligned with the orientation of the wooden remains found in the previous tumulus. Basil noted that, again, there were signs of disturbances by rabbits, as well as other possible human digging, but the following day some pieces of iron were discovered – "One was certainly the remnant of a ship rivet, much corroded."

Convinced already that he had uncovered a ship burial, Basil wrote to May back at home in Rickinghall on Friday 15 July: "The evidence obtained so far as we have gone in the big mound is that the chief was buried in his ship, very probably about 50 feet in length but the remains are many iron rivets and iron bands and some especially fine pieces of glass." He also asked Guy Maynard to send him details of an earlier ship burial discovery at nearby Snape and the following Wednesday, Bill Lyons took Basil to Aldeburgh Museum to examine the relics and rivets from the Snape ship, which Basil observed were "very like those at Sutton Hoo, so it will be advisable to keep these finds in mind as the only ones of the Anglo-Saxon period in Suffolk." In a letter to his wife on 21 July, he describes the Sutton Hoo rivets as nearly twice the size of those found at Snape. Basil looked for and found a boat to accompany his rivets and the base of the burial pit was "boat-shaped without any question" with some of the rivets still *in situ*. Yet again, though, this mound appeared to have been plundered and scraps of

Basil's photo of the spoil heaps from Tumulus D, later Mound 2 (SCCAS)

Basil's photo of Tumulus E, later Mound 4, at sunrise (SCCAS)

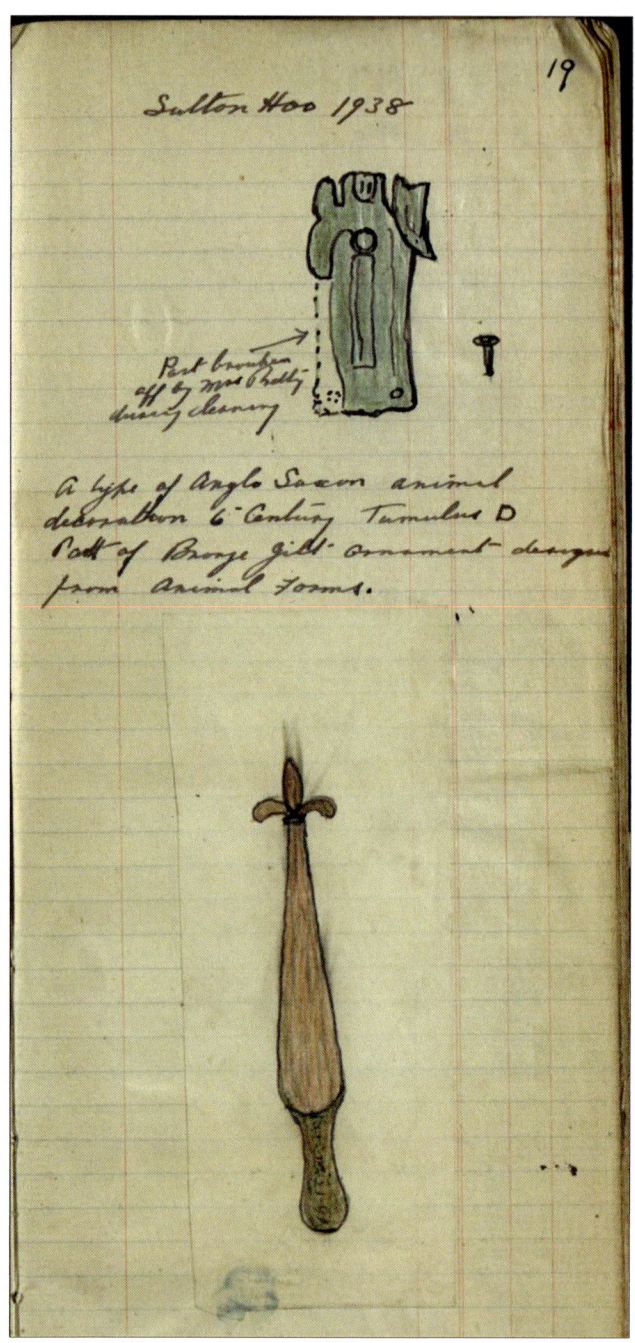

A page from Basil Brown Archive volume XIII (SCCAS)

finds were found at the base of the ship, including small fragments of a blue glass vessel and a number of bronze items such as a buckle and a brooch.

Between 30 July and 9 August, Basil excavated a third mound (his Tumulus E, later Mound 4) where: "The burial pit contained many fragments of thin bronze evidently belonging to a vessel of thin bronze which had been smashed. It had most likely contained the bones from a cremation burial. These may have been wrapped in a linen cloth or textile of some kind for we found pieces of textile were adhering to the fragments of the bronze vessel. The calcined bones appeared to be those of a young man."

A difficult relationship with the Ipswich Museum
Basil returned home to Rickinghall on Tuesday 9 August and restarted his work on the Stanton Chare Roman villa dig the following day. During his seven weeks or so at Sutton Hoo, Basil had excavated three previously robbed barrows which contained little in the way of real treasure. However, his early identification of a ship burial in Mound 3 and then rivets in Mound 2, drawing on his wide reading over many years, demonstrated Basil's sound archaeological credentials. In fact, in his later (undated) *Notes by B Brown on S H*, Basil gives himself due credit for the later Great Ship Burial discovery, saying: "It will now be seen that the clues and deductions of 1938 were the dominating factors from which this burial ship of the 7th century AD came to light in 1939."[2] However, his abilities as an excavator were questioned by some at the Ipswich Museum from time to time.

A lengthy entry in Basil's diary dated Tuesday 26 July relates to a visit made to Sutton Hoo by Harold Spencer. Spencer was an assistant at the museum and claimed he had originally been asked to supervise the dig. A heated discussion ensued between Harold Spencer and Basil Brown in which (according to Basil's diary): "The assistant from the Museum told me that I did not know about the soils in that part of the county, and I strongly objected to this statement." This "bother", as Basil put it, was smoothed over thanks to the intervention of Mrs Pretty and work continued. James Reid-Moir, President of the Ipswich Museum, was also critical of Basil Brown at times, believing that Basil was too quick to draw conclusions from his findings. Reid-Moir visited the dig on 13 July and, as Basil records: "Apparently he does not yet believe in the pits or graves beneath the mounds for he shouted out to me, 'That's not the way to do it, Brown', but Mrs Pretty made no remark and provided Mrs Pretty gives no special directions, I will take advice or help only if it is useful from the Museum officials or anyone else, but I've decided I will go home rather than be dictated to, if I am certain of being right re graves beneath the mounds." There is no doubt that Basil had the courage of his own convictions and that he was prepared to fight his corner.

Return to Sutton Hoo
It was two short messages from Guy Maynard at the Ipswich Museum that ultimately led to Basil's momentous discovery in 1939. The first was a letter dated 14 April that year which began: "If you would like another spell at Sutton Hoo, Mrs Pretty is willing to resume work on the barrows." The second was a brief telegram sent to Basil on 6 May which read "Start Sutton Hoo work on Monday."[3] So, on Monday 8 May 1939, having left his luggage at the Lyon's house in Bromeswell (where he was to lodge once again) and after a walk to the mounds and subsequent consultation with Mrs Pretty, Basil embarked on his excavation of Mound 1 (his Tumulus I), digging a trench six feet wide, running east to west, together with two new helpers.

A rather wonderful letter survives written by Rupert Bruce-Mitford at the British Museum to Basil.[4] It reads: "I seem to remember your telling me that the 1939 Sutton Hoo dig was nearly called off because of Mrs Pretty's chrysanthemums or gladioli or something. You said that you would have to stop, if you were going to get these flowers planted out in time, as arranged. Mrs Pretty, after thinking it over, said she was sure there was something good in the burial, and hang the gladioli. Would you kindly give me the true facts of this occurrence?"

Sadly, we may never know whether this story was true. However, in his diary entry for the day of his arrival at Sutton Hoo, Basil records that although Mrs Pretty offered William Spooner, her gamekeeper, and John Jacobs, the gardener at Little Sutton, to help with the dig that year: "Spooner was ready to begin but Jacobs was in the garden and not able to come till the following morning." It may be, therefore, that the gardener had to complete the planting before assisting.

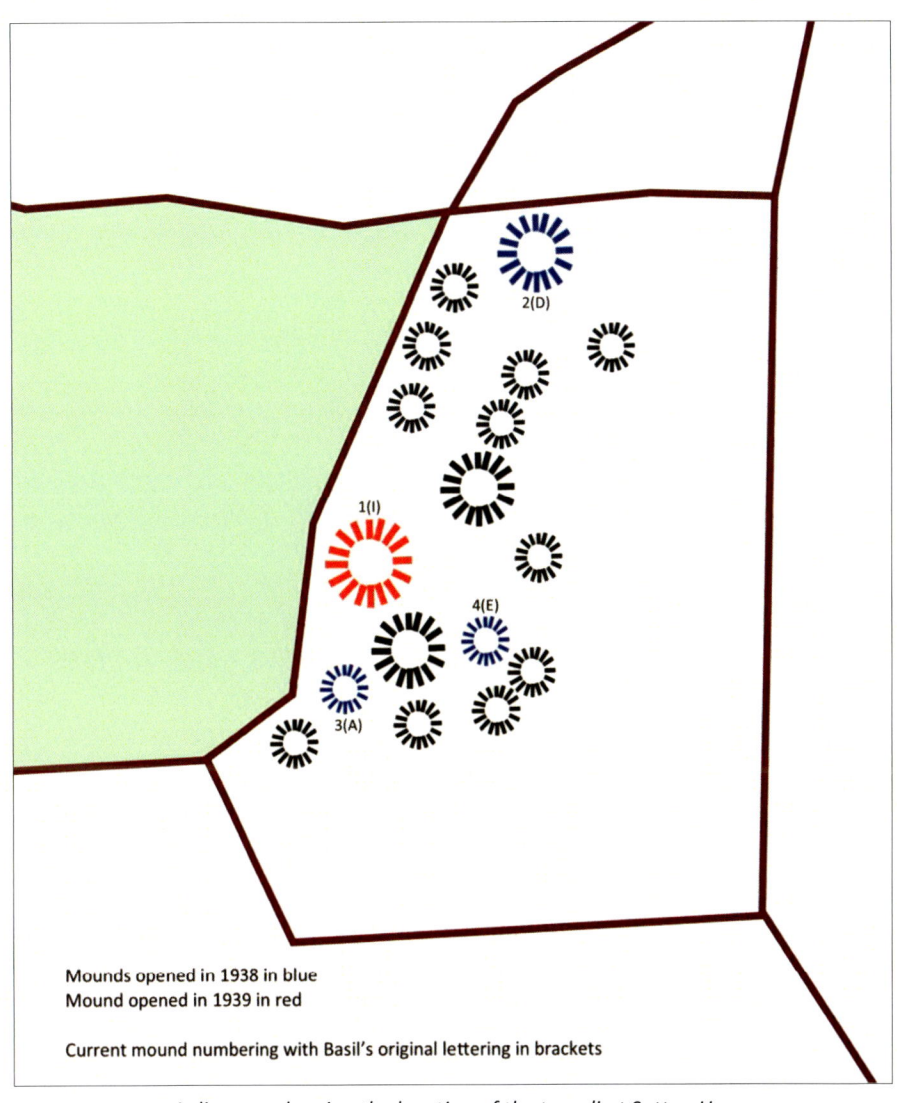

*A diagram showing the location of the tumuli at Sutton Hoo
(adapted from Amitchell125 at English Wikipedia
under Creative Commons Attribution 3.0 Unported license)*

The Great Ship Burial is uncovered

Progress on the barrow was swift and a matter of days after starting the dig, on Thursday 11 May, Basil records: "About mid-day Jacobs, who by the way had never seen a ship rivet before and being for the first time engaged in excavation work, called out he had found a piece of iron, afterwards found to be a loose one at the end of a ship. I immediately stopped the work and carefully explored the area with a small trowel and uncovered five rivets in position on what turned out to be the extreme end prow or stern of a ship."

The next day, Basil wrote to May telling her about the finds, quite astonishingly beginning his letter "I've not much news" but then continuing: "We get several falls owing to disturbance by rabbits, etc. but I have reached many ship rivets spaced 4½ inches, so it appears to have had another ship burial, but is large enough to contain two fair sized narrow ships which the Danes used in the 8th century AD. Bits of charred wood (oak) from the timbers of the ship are found where we are digging now, so there ought to be objects when we get about 15 feet down." [5]

Basil wrote a further letter to his wife on the Sunday, saying: "Shall most likely reach the burial tomorrow. It's there alright but whether there is anything special or not, I can't tell, but there ought to be considering the hill is like a small mountain and the mounds are over burials of chiefs. But one or other may have been over a personage of high standing." May replied to her husband the following Monday, writing rather prophetically "Hope you have good finds today. It would be nice to come across something really good and uncommon."

Over the next two weeks, Basil Brown, John Jacobs and William Spooner continued to widen the trench, uncovering more of the outline of the ship as defined by the lines of rivets. Basil recorded that the vessel was located some 20 feet below the top of the barrow and on 18 May, Basil noted: "Clearing ship with small tools and hands as much as possible owing to the head of each rivet has to be found and cleared … Am unable to let the men do this work owing to the risk of damage and they are getting on with the widening of the trench."

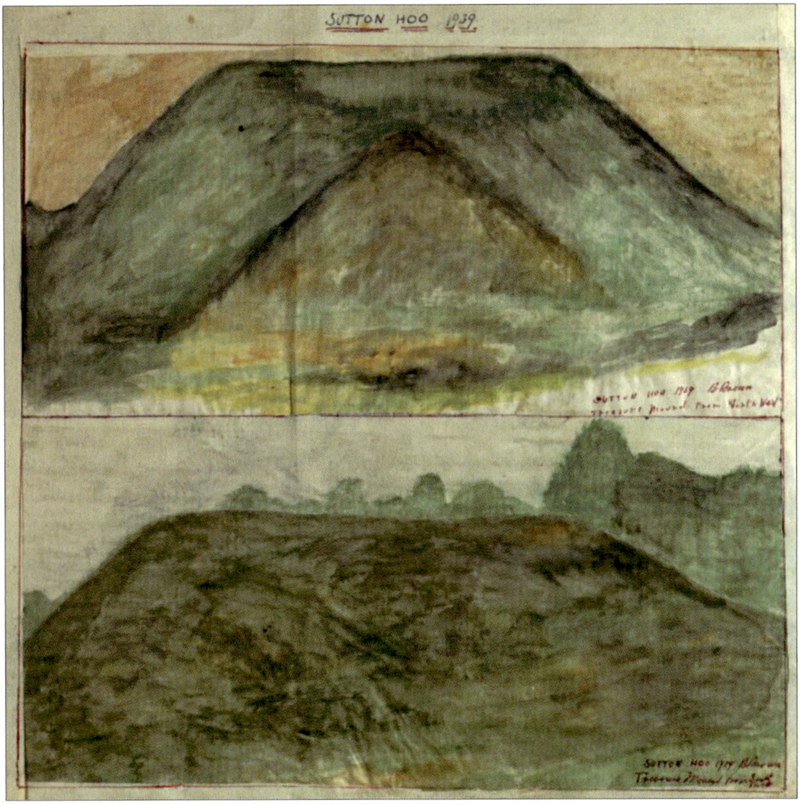

Basil's own watercolours from Basil Brown Archive volume XCVI (SCCAS)

The following Monday, Basil wrote to May: "Mr Maynard was over Friday and agreed that the find is most important and such a find is unique in this country (ship burials have of course been found but not as good as this)." By now, Basil was aware of the importance of this discovery and ensured that photos and drawings of the excavated parts of the ship were taken in case of, as he put it in his diary "anything going wrong", by that he must have meant the ever-present threat of landslides which he was seeking to prevent by shoring up the sides with timber planks.

As the Whitsun holiday approached, excitement at Sutton Hoo was building. Edith Pretty cancelled her travel plans, staying put on her estate instead. According to Basil's diary, she had been getting increasingly keen to reach the burial for some time. Basil, however, managed to get home for a couple of days, leaving William Spooner "in charge of the site re possible visitors or trespassers." It seems that Basil did not take it easy in Rickinghall because shortly after his return to Sutton Hoo he wrote to May: "Hope weeds are dead in garden and chrysanthemums alive." Basil and his assistants resumed their work although two landslides in quick succession - one, according to Basil's account, missing him by a few minutes - hindered any further progress towards the burial.

On 2 June, James Reid-Moir visited the dig, accompanied by the Financial Secretary of the Suffolk Institute of Archaeology and History. This year, unlike a previous visit from Reid-Moir on 23 May, there was no disagreement between the Ipswich Museum President and Basil. In fact, Mr Reid-Moir agreed with Basil's assessment that the cutting should be further widened before an attempt to dig any further down in search of the burial chamber.

Charles Phillips visits and takes charge
It was on Tuesday 6 June at around lunchtime when Guy Maynard arrived on site with Charles Phillips, a historian, archaeologist and fellow of Selwyn College, Cambridge. Phillips had been alerted to the Sutton Hoo finds via the archaeological rumour mill. In his letter to May that evening, Basil writes that Charles Phillips: "Was so surprised, declared it was on a scale with the big ships found in Norway, Sweden and Denmark and might go outside the mound. May be the ship of one of the kings and it was a find of

national importance but acknowledged my excavation had been perfect and could not have been better done."

Three days later, Phillips returned with an official from the Office of Works, a representative sent by the British Museum, together with Basil's superiors from the Ipswich Museum. All the visitors were, according to Basil's letter home the same day "very complimentary at the way it had been cleared. In fact, I think they were all surprised that it was possible for it to be done so well."

The experts returned to their respective desks to consider how best to proceed with the dig with a more experienced team and although some accounts of the 1939 excavation suggest that Basil was instructed to stop excavating at this point, this order was certainly not recorded by Basil in his diary.[6] In fact, Basil writes: "The decision eventually arrived at was to cover the portion excavated with Hessian etc., and fill it in with sand until a shed could be put over it, and the excavation of the other part of the ship to continue as before." So, over the next four weeks, Basil continued his careful work, now convinced that the burial chamber remained intact.

According to Basil's diary, Mrs Pretty seemed keen for him to reach the burial chamber, but he proceeded with the utmost caution. His diary entry for Monday 19 June does record that he had heard that further excavation was to be suspended until the planned shed was erected, although work appears to have continued. On 29 June, Basil wrote to his wife: "I have found the other end of the ship. About 84 feet from one end to the other … It must have been the ship of a king or person of very great importance for one of the largest warships of the time to be used."

On Monday 10 July, Charles Phillips arrived at Sutton Hoo and, as Basil recorded in his diary that day: "Phillips will apparently act as representative of the Office of Works here so he will keep his own log. Anyway I shall not have so much bother and responsibility now in case anything went wrong. I think we shall be able to co-operate all right, at least I hope so … I am to be his assistant, but still in the employ of Mrs Pretty." The following day, his account records that there was an argument on site between Guy Maynard and Charles Phillips which resulted in the Ipswich Museum stepping back from any further involvement. He writes: "I have decided to be neutral in

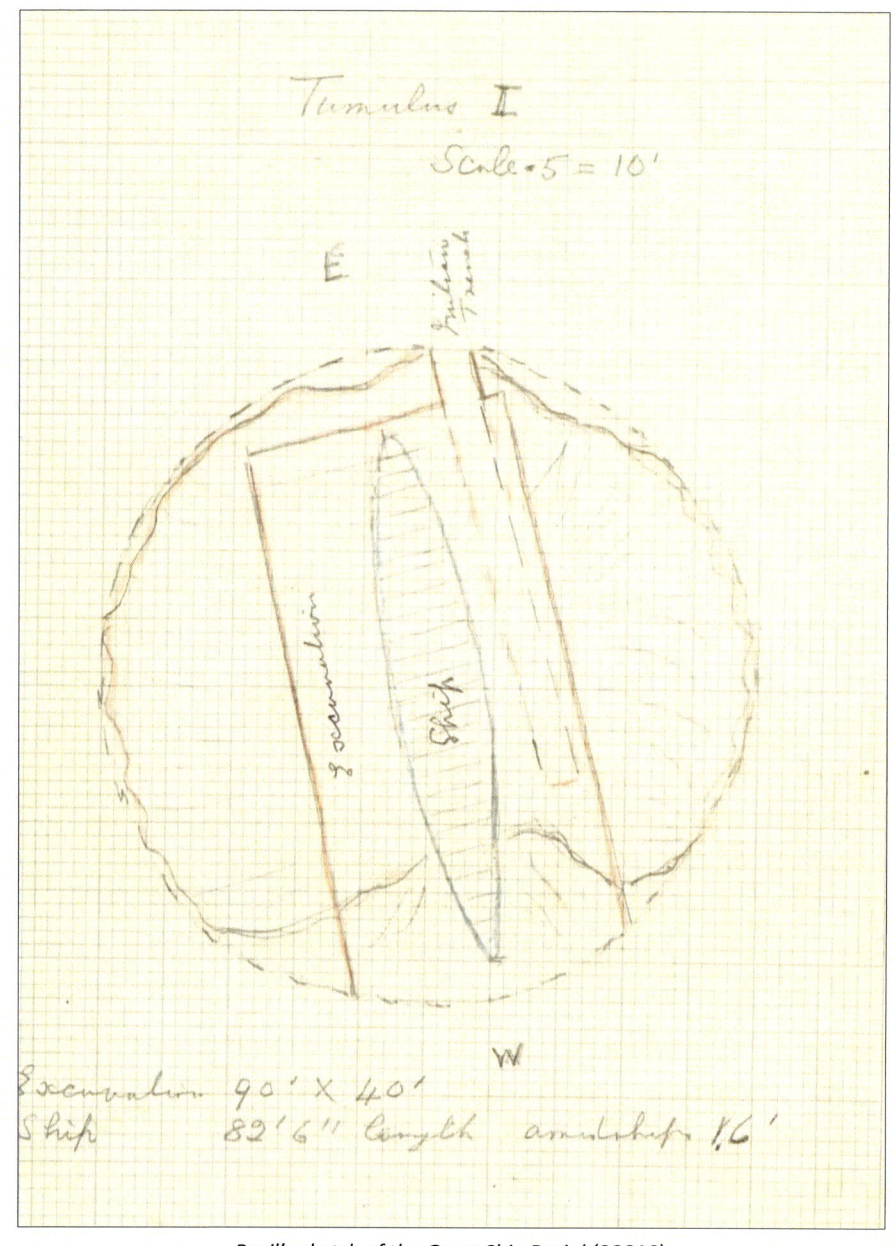

Basil's sketch of the Great Ship Burial (SCCAS)

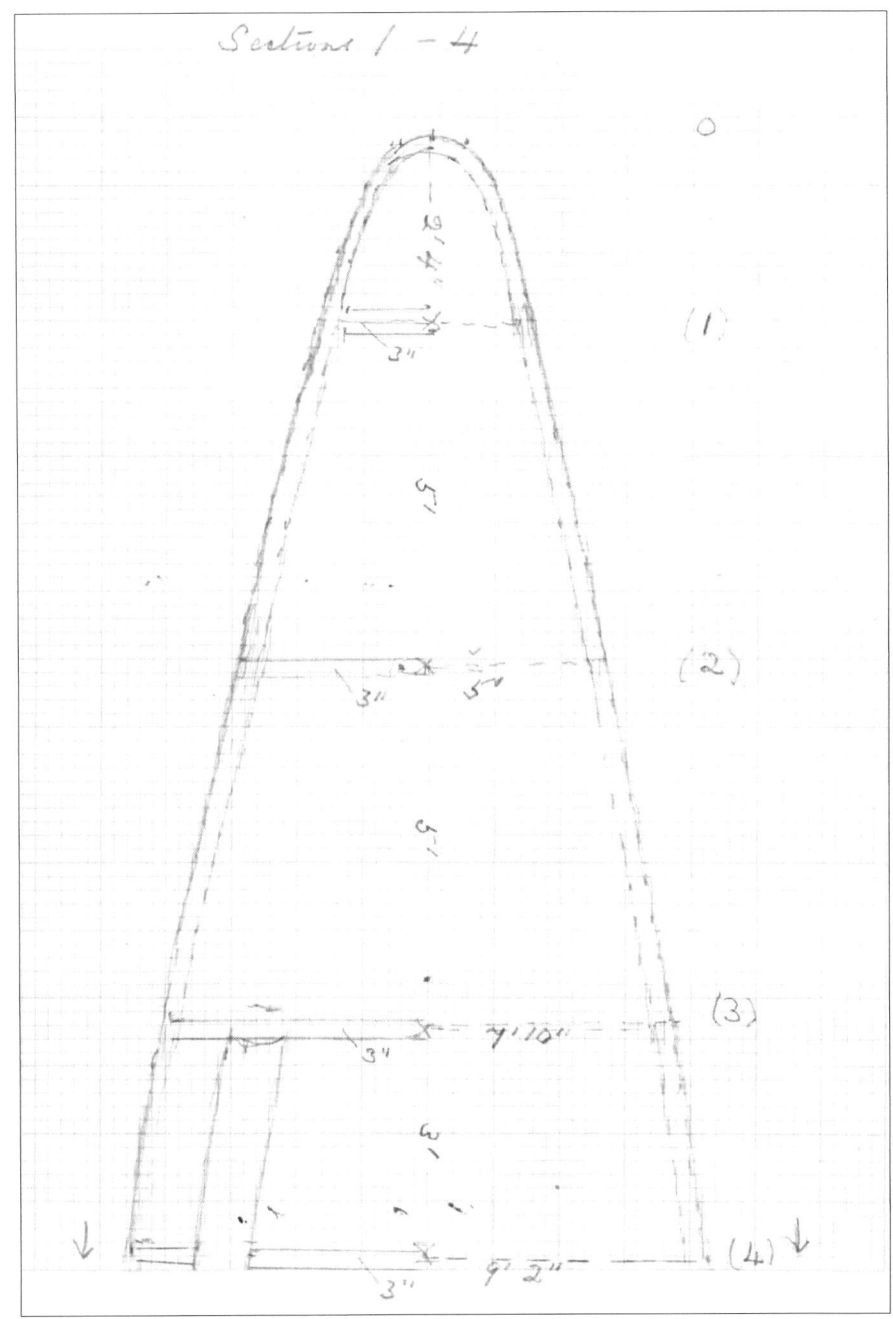

Basil's sketch of the Great Ship Burial (SCCAS)

all disputes but as the employee of Mrs Pretty I should carry out any suggestions or orders she might express." Privately, Basil wrote to May: "Phillips seems to be alright ... [he] made me a present of nearly a week's supply of tobacco today."[7]

Indeed, the relationship between Phillips and Basil, of which much has been written since 1939, seemed to be one of mutual respect. Phillips writes of Basil's work prior to his own involvement: "It was here that his decision not to go blindly on digging into the mound made a major contribution to the success of the whole 1939 excavation."[8] After Sutton Hoo, Charles Phillips and Basil Brown continued to correspond sporadically; the tone friendly. Writing to Basil in December 1972 of his latest news and good wishes for the New Year, Phillips ends: "Well, a good job was done in 1939, and not least by you. That is a fact which cannot be got over, whatever happens, and it will be many a long day before anything to compare with it turns up in Britain, if ever."[9]

The burial is reached
Charles Phillips and his hastily assembled team of friends and colleagues, including Stuart and Peggy Piggott, soon made progress and as Basil reports to May on 13 July: "Burial opened Monday, I should say in fact we are only about 6 inches above but as I expected, the burial chamber is crushed and the objects are a bit mixed up." Again, contrary to popular belief, Basil was not sidelined altogether. His diary entry for Monday 17 July records: "I have today uncovered the portion of the burial which I found on June 14th at Phillips suggestion as he says that I know most about it." The following day Basil's letter back home records: "Still very busy. I don't know exactly what we have in the burial yet. There is a lot to be done to clear the burial objects. Work has to be very slow owing to their crushed condition and several large iron objects and wood in quite good condition. Perhaps a large bronze cauldron or maybe a shield underneath or possibly a box. I expect we shall have to go back to my original theory of last year however and the ship is Anglo Saxon instead of Viking."

The treasure emerges from the soil
It was on Friday 21 July that Peggy Piggott uncovered the first piece of jewellery; a small, gold and garnet pyramidal strap mount and Basil's diary records a heightened excitement at Sutton Hoo. Even before this, though,

Edith Pretty had decided to host a large garden party on Tuesday 25 July during which her guests would be able to view the "Viking Ship", as she described it then. Guy Maynard wrote to Basil on 19 July saying: "Mrs Pretty told me that she would like you to be amongst the people next Tuesday and have your best clothes and I said I would mention it to you … P.S. If there is anything I can do for you re the clothes question please don't hesitate to come over or let me know."[10]

The following day, Basil wrote to his wife: "Mrs Pretty is of course having a large garden party, over 300 invitations being sent out today I hear, and a first class band is to play on Tuesday. Mrs Pretty has asked if I've my best suit here so I suppose I shall have to go in style. Most of the prominent people are being invited including Lord Ullswater, at one time Speaker of the House of Commons. On the other part, the government are attaching a very great importance to the ship, so much so that Phillips said he believed he'd jump in the Deben if anything happened."

Sherry on the lawn
Edith Pretty's sherry party on the evening of Tuesday 25 July turned out very differently than she had originally envisaged. In the time between the invitations "to view remains of Viking ship burial" had been issued, and the day of the event itself, the Sutton Hoo Great Ship Burial treasure had been uncovered; the first burial items by Peggy Piggott and then more objects in the following 24 hours or so.[11] Basil wrote to May: "The actual burial was reached today and under a large silver dish were bowls, textiles, silver and bronze objects which date burial about 600 AD or a little later. Looking down I saw a lovely gold and jewelled ornament through the field glasses."

Mrs Pretty arranged, at her own expense, for the burial site to be guarded, night and day, by members of the local police force. Each valuable item was carefully extracted from the ground by the team and packed into boxes. In a typed account entitled "Echoes of the Sutton Hoo Excavations", Basil later wrote: "I had the honour of carrying much of the gold to the mansion for Mrs Pretty said 'Brown will carry it in' and we walked from the mound to the house with Spencer the gamekeeper with his gun following and so the finest of the gold objects left the mound after lying for centuries beneath it."[12] The treasure was removed in batches to the British Museum in London for safekeeping.

So, although Mrs Pretty's guests were treated to a visit to the dig site after their drinks, as well as a short talk from Charles Phillips about the discovery of the ship burial, the dig team found themselves under immense pressure to keep details of the extraordinary finds secret until press coverage could be properly managed. Invited correspondents from the *East Anglian Daily Times* were there but there were no official briefings about the treasure finds.

However, the party also saw relations between Charles Phillips and Guy Maynard flare up once again. Maynard was apparently annoyed that Phillips had not mentioned the role of Ipswich Museum in the excavations. Added to this was the fact that Maynard was 'ordered off Suffolk soil' when he tried to take some guests to view the ship: following some rain, there was a risk of landslides and so the prepared viewing platform was deemed unsafe and so this was not the personal sleight perceived by Maynard. Nevertheless, this argument led to the leaking of the story of treasure at the ship burial to the press and it was on Saturday 29 July that the *East Anglian Daily Times* printed full coverage of the find. The same day, Basil wrote home: "The news should not have leaked out, but apparently the dispute between the British Museum and Ipswich came to a head by Maynard or Ipswich Museum officials letting go the whole thing at an awkward time."

The following week, Basil wrote further to May on the subject: "This left me in a very difficult position between two or three very powerful forces ... I have remained neutral until yesterday, taking no sides, acknowledging no employer but Mrs Pretty." Of the press coverage, Basil continued: "Personalities are mentioned as little as possible but I expect Ipswich will explode, especially if they wanted to claim some of the treasure by making me out to be their foreman ... The strain on everyone, including myself, has been very great. I shall be glad of some rest anyway... Bother the inquest! If the find is declared treasure trove, it will go to the Crown and full value will go to Mrs Pretty. If not, Mrs Pretty will have it and may present it to the Nation. I am afraid Ipswich have done themselves a great deal of harm – we shall see."

Basil at Sutton Hoo in 1939 (SCCAS)

The inquest

By the time the Coroner's Inquest was convened on Monday 14 August in the village hall in the nearby village of Sutton, public interest in the treasure hoard had reached fever pitch. On the day before the inquest, Basil wrote a long letter (for him) to his wife back in Rickinghall telling her that: "Ipswich is keeping the E.A.D.T. and some of the papers going with stuff but whether they will benefit by this, I don't know. The Government side are saying little at present. Neither am I ... This month's East Anglian Magazine says – The first is that the greater part of the glory which shines so abundantly over the whole discovery belongs in the main to three people. Mrs. E. M. Pretty who owns the Sutton Hoo estate and who has borne their entire cost; Mr. Guy Maynard, Curator of the Ipswich Museum, who has given the authority of his experience to the excavations since they were first contemplated last year and who has shouldered most of the responsibility and Mr. Basil Brown, of whom it might be said that no excavation in Suffolk attains to perfection unless he is on the spot to take charge of the work."

Basil's witness statement to the inquest was relatively short and, like the rest of the proceedings, it was listened to not only by those present in the small hall, but also by a large crowd gathered outside thanks to the BBC. That evening, the recording was broadcast on the radio to the wider public. The result of the inquest was published in the press the next day; the items were judged not to be Treasure Trove and were deemed to belong to their first finder, Mrs Pretty who did, indeed, decide to donate the Sutton Hoo treasure to the nation.

Preparing for war

After a constant stream of visitors to the burial site since the news had broken in the papers, Edith Pretty closed her estate to the general public from 16 August, intending a special open day. As Basil wrote in his letter to May on 25 August (the day Charles Phillips left Sutton Hoo): "We are getting the ship ready for visitors to see it Sept, 2nd or 3rd but the situation may upset this." The situation to which he was referring was, of course, the growing inevitability of war with Germany.

Basil's photo of the ferry from Woodbridge to Sutton (SCCAS)

Basil's photo Mr & Mrs Cannell and May Brown visiting Sutton Hoo (SCCAS)

In the meantime, Basil continued his support work with residual excavation and tidying of the ship burial. Several VIP guests were shown around by Edith Pretty, including Princess Marie Louise, Duchess of Argyll. One other special guest who was allowed to visit was May Brown who was driven down from Rickinghall by Mr and Mrs Cannell, friends of the Browns. Writing to her husband the day after her visit, May says that she "greatly enjoyed our outing", describing the ship burial as "a lovely thing." War was declared on Sunday 3 September 1939 and Basil, assisted by William Spooner, started covering the lines of rivets with hessian and filling in the interior with dry bracken, so that the ship might be preserved during the conflict.

Spiritualism
Edith Pretty was interested in Spiritualism; a popular movement in the 1930s. Spiritualists believed that the spirits of the dead had both the ability and the desire to communicate with the living. Mrs Pretty's links with the Spiritualists were particularly strong during her husband's illness and after his subsequent death in December 1934. At this time, Alfred Scarfe ran a Spiritualist church at a hall at the back of a house in New Street, Woodbridge and although Edith gave regular financial support to the local Spiritualist church in Woodbridge, she never attended meetings there.[13] Instead, on her frequent visits to London, she went to Spiritualist gatherings and formed a lasting friendship with well-known faith healers.[14]

There has been a long-held theory that Edith Pretty decided to have the burial mounds on her property investigated because of a ghostly vision she, or one of her friends, was supposed to have seen. In 1954, the Honorary Secretary of The Speleological Society (a national body for those interested in the study and exploration of caves) wrote to Basil having first approached Norman Smedley and Guy Maynard. On behalf of his members, the secretary wrote: "We have been intrigued with a story that originally Mrs Pretty was influenced by a vision or dream which was interpreted by the Spiritualistic Circle in Woodbridge … If you can give me any information regarding clairvoyance having assisted in your wonderful effort, I shall be most grateful if you will pass it on."[15] Basil's reply essentially dismisses this theory, and his words could be viewed as the most authoritative on the matter. He wrote:

"Few know exactly what really happened I expect! And it is rather a long story so I will be brief but shall be pleased to amplify any time. Mrs Pretty's vision of a procession of white robed priests etc has little truth as far as I am aware."

This view is reinforced in an account Basil wrote about his Sutton Hoo dig, in which he recorded:

"A story is even now current in some quarters that Mrs Pretty had a vision of a burial procession with white robed priests wending its way to the burial mounds but the truth is more prosaic and very few had heard of her interest in archaeological excavation before even the Sutton Hoo estate was purchased, of a dig at the monastic site in Cheshire while at Vale Royal. Therefore when she became the owner of an estate with a group of mounds marked Tumuli on OS sheet she speculated whether they really were burial mounds."[16]

It is now well known that Edith Pretty had witnessed several archaeological excavations as a young lady, including at her parents' home at Vale Royal in Cheshire. So, much as the tale of the vision is a romantic one, it does seem as if this was not true.

The enquiry from The Speleological Society, however, also elicited the following reply from Basil:

"Later happenings are authentic as what happened to me in the hall used by the Woodbridge Spiritualists. Furthermore it appears to have had some effect on the dig. At this time there was a serious attempt to hold up the dig by certain individuals who wanted to control the excavations."

From the surviving letters sent between Basil and May, we know that the Browns were interested in Spiritualism at this time, and that Edith Pretty encouraged Basil's attendance at the local meetings in Woodbridge.[17] May's letters to Basil indicate that she, too, encouraged her husband's interest in such matters. Frustratingly, we know only a fraction of what transpired at the meetings Basil attended: the references in his letters often suggested that he would brief his wife fully when he returned home on his regular visits.

For instance, on 22 May 1939 he wrote: "Have been to 3 Spiritualist meetings but what transpired must wait till I come home" and three days later his letter said "I only had a mental question answered by medium on Sunday night. She certainly hit the mark very well." In Basil's letter of 6 June, however, we get a little more information:

"I went on Sunday evening but I don't know whether the medium had any idea, was a thought reader or what - or genuine or not - Mrs Gilbert of London. Here is a bit. 'I'm coming to the gentleman in the corner. I see fields, meadows, etc. Were you or your people ever connected with the land. Yes. Now I see land everywhere (spreading her hands). I see a most beautiful vision. You have nothing to fear from any source. You broke away from the land for something high and more important and everything is alright.' Nobody else in the room got anything so nice, mostly the reverse."

Basil also reported to May the further message received on 2 July and a typed, signed account by Basil gives us a first-hand account of this incident; the one to which Basil refers in his reply to The Speleological Society.[18] He stated:

"On Sunday July 2nd 1939 I went to a meeting at the Woodbridge Spiritualist Church. The medium was Mrs Florence Thompson of London. There was a large congregation present and I slipped in quietly and rather late and got a seat in the extreme right hand corner of the hall where I was not likely to be noticed. After the usual prayers, singing of Hymns and an address, the medium walked across the platform and said that she was coming to the gentleman in the corner, so I prepared to answer questions. Mrs Thompson was very positive in what she said. THE MESSAGE. I see green fields which you left for a more important position ... Now I see lots of sand ... all sand ... and then she spread her arms to emphasise this ... Now someone is holding you up in your business ... ASSERT YOURSELF ... go on digging and you will find what you are looking for."

Spiritualists in Rickinghall

It perhaps not surprising, given the popularity of the movement at this time, to find practising Spiritualists in the Rickinghall area. Basil's report to his wife of what Florence Thompson had said to him included the line "Now if Mr Whitmore wants a medium, he should get Mrs Thompson at his next meeting." In other letters to May, Basil mentions two other London mediums - Mrs Gilbert and Mrs Austin - who were at meetings he attended in Woodbridge, and he suggests that Mr Whitmore may know of them. Of Mrs Austin, who Basil thought was impressive, he wrote "She might cause a bit of thinking if she visited Botesdale."

Basil's letter of 24 June, whilst reporting that he had had no message at the last Spiritualist meeting he attended, asked May to thank Mr Whitmore for his letter and for the information in it. In return, Basil asked her to pass on to Whitmore details of a publisher of Spiritualist hymn books. Mr Robert A Whitmore lived in The Uplands in Rickinghall in the 1920s and 30s and is described in the National Register of 1939 as of independent means.[19] Robert Whitmore appears to have changed his surname from Slipper sometime before his move to Rickinghall. Under his former name, he had served as a Church of England clergyman, including in at least two parishes as curate to his father who was the rector. A report in the *Diss Express* of 24 March 1939 shows that both Whitmore and Basil were leading lights in the local Spiritualist movement, proposing and seconding, respectively, a vote of thanks for the visiting speakers who had given an address on 'After death what?' at a recent meeting held at the Bell Hotel Assembly Room, after which a demonstration of clairvoyance was held.

On 8 September 1934, the *Eastern Daily Press* published a letter from Mr Whitmore, entitled "A Metrical Study in ABC" which demonstrates his high regard for Basil and his abilities even in these early days of Basil's archaeological career.[20] His letter refers to a verse published some 80 years previously about the siege of Belgrade in which each line, and each word within the line, starts with a fresh letter of the alphabet. Whitmore says: "The other evening, with my mind full of the fresh discoveries made by our indefatigable local savant, Mr Basil Brown, and his enthusiastic friends, in Cork Wood, Rickinghall, and the neighbourhood ... I started an imitation of the above-mentioned metrical curiosity." This is followed by Robert Whitmore's literary homage to Basil which reads:

An antient[21] arrow Anglian art attained,
Bared by Brown (Basil), bountifully brained,
Cork copses cover ceramic correct –
Determined diggers' daily "dibs" detect –

Each early English evidence entails
Fine fistic fortitude, for faintness fails,
Gents gently gather great geologic gems,
Historic humus, hole, or high hill hems,
Increased instructive insight intermingles –
Jaws jostle jugs, jars jostling joblots jingles –
Keen, kindly kinsmen, Keltic kiosks know
Learned look localizes limbs lying low,
Mounds most mysterious mankind manifest
Nigh neolithic nameless natives' nest,
Opening or observing objects overlaid,
Prototypic pottery perseverance paid,
Quizzing, quoting, questioning, quiet quarries quaint,
Roman records reading, retrospects repaint;
Seeking Saxon scarcities science seldom sees,
Tracing time-worn thigh-bones, "tuskers" touching trees,
"Upchurch" urns upheaving, unscathed, unsurpassed,
Villas, vallums, vases, value very vast,
Worthy well with wonders, working wisest wight,
X-rays, xylobalsam, xenium, xylonite,
Yearning youthful yeomen, yawning yesternight,
Zealously zetetic, zoning zoolite.

Departure from Sutton Hoo
On 2 August 1939, on the eve of the outbreak of the Second World War, May Brown wrote to Edith Pretty:
> "I feel I must write and tell you how pleased I am to think that such an important find has been found on your estate and I thank you from the bottom of my heart for your great kindness in giving my dear husband this work to do. I know how delighted he is and it is the work he loves. How proud his dear parents would be ... I always ask for guidance in my husband's work and it has been granted."[22]

At the age of fifty-one, Basil Brown had reached the pinnacle of his chosen career and had been instrumental in uncovering what has been described as the greatest single discovery in the annals of English archaeology. As he put it in one of his letters to his wife: "It is a find of a lifetime."[23] It revolutionised how historians viewed and understood the Anglo-Saxon era.

At the time it was also dubbed "Britain's Tutankhamen", a term that would not have been lost on Basil who had his early scrapbooks sitting at home in Rickinghall into which he had pasted cuttings of the discovery of the pharaoh's tomb. We can therefore, perhaps, forgive him for having kept a particularly significant memento of his Sutton Hoo excavation. In one of Basil's notebooks is a brief, scribbled note which might easily be overlooked by those glancing through its pages. It is headed "Specimens in Workshop", which is highly likely to have meant the sheds in his garden at Cambria, and at the bottom of a short list of items are the words "S H Ship Rivets 1939 (Bent)".[24]

---

[1] A full transcription of Basil Brown's diary of his 1938 and 1939 (to 11 July only) Sutton Hoo excavations is published in Bruce-Mitford, 1974. Basil's original diary covering this period is in the British Museum. A typescript transcript of Basil's diary entries from 12 July onwards is held in Basil Brown Archive volume LXIV and LXIVa (SA/I: HD 3096/5/28). I have drawn on these transcriptions throughout this chapter.
[2] Basil Brown Archive volume VII (SA/I: HD 3096/1/6).
[3] Basil records both messages, in full, in his diary.
[4] Held by the SSCAS.
[5] Basil Brown Archive volume VII (SA/I: HD 3096/1/6) contains copies, transcribed by hand by Basil himself, of letters he wrote to May during his time at Sutton Hoo. The same volume also contains letters from May to Basil, all sadly undated but some can be roughly dated from their contents. I quote from these letters throughout this chapter.
[6] Carver, 1998.
[7] His letter dated 11 July 1939 in Basil Brown Archive volume VII (SA/I: HD 3096/1/6).
[8] Phillips, 1987.
[9] Several original typed and handwritten letters from Charles Phillips are to be found in Basil Brown Archive volume VII held by the SCCAS.
[10] Several typed and handwritten letters from Guy Maynard are to be found in Basil Brown Archive volume VII held by the SCCAS.
[11] A copy of the invitation to the party is reproduced in Markham, 2002.
[12] These notes are to be found in Basil Brown Archive volume VII held by the SCCAS.
[13] Notes made by Simon Peachey from an interview with Sheila Norman, daughter of Alfred Scarfe, in July 2022, as well as printed material from Mrs Norman relating to the Spiritualist church in Woodbridge are at NT SH/RF1/SEC/DOC/24.

[14] Skelcher, 2006.
[15] This letter and a copy of Basil's reply (and draft reply) are in the copy of Basil Brown Archive volume VII held by the SCCAS.
[16] This is drawn from a heavily edited first draft of this account appears in Basil Brown Archive volume LI (SA/I: Accession No. 18855). In Basil's final version, he omits (by mistake, I believe) the wording after "Cheshire".
[17] Basil Brown Archive volume VII (SA/I: HD 3096/1/6).
[18] NT SH/RF1/SEC/DOC/24.
[19] TNA: RG101/6644D/002/27.
[20] A newspaper cutting of this letter is to be found at NT SH/BB1/PRIM/DOC/12.
[21] According to several online dictionaries, "antient" is an obsolete spelling of "ancient".
[22] NT SH/EP2/PRIM/DOC/9a.
[23] His letter dated 29 June 1939 in Basil Brown Archive volume VII (SA/I: HD 3096/1/6).
[24] Basil Brown Archive volume XL (SA/I: Accession No. 18855).

Chapter 6
The War Years

"One can only make the best of a bad job"

It is hard to imagine just what an anti-climax it must have been for Basil Brown on the eve of the Second World War, having just witnessed the magnificent Sutton Hoo treasure being transported off to the British Museum for safekeeping. In a letter to his wife on 3 September, the day that British Prime Minister, Neville Chamberlain, declared war on Germany, Basil wrote:

"Hope you are alright in all this bother of war being declared. I am today filling in the ship with Bracken etc and hope it will remain alright. Then if war does not last too long, it may come out alright for people to see. If not it must take its chance. I don't know where I am at present. Mrs Pretty even now thinks the war will fizzle out in a short time, but while Hitler is alive anything may happen, and air raids are the danger."

He was facing an uncertain future like many others across the nation. The following day, Basil said in his letter home: "I hope this war will be over soon but we may be in for a long one, but one can only make the best of a bad job."[1]

Job seeking

Finding employment after Sutton Hoo had clearly been foremost in his mind for some time. On 18 August, Basil had written optimistically to May: "I quite think if I don't get work in one quarter, I shall in another." His position at the Ipswich Museum had been a casual one and for the duration of the Sutton Hoo dig, Basil was considered Edith Pretty's employee. In his letter home on 11 September, he reports on a "somewhat heated discussion" with Guy Maynard at the Ipswich Museum, whom he had stopped off to see on his way back to Sutton Hoo after a weekend in Rickinghall. His letter continues:

"I said I wanted something permanent as I hated the unemployment and might as well stop where I am. He said he was not the Guy Maynard he used to be and I said, neither was I the Basil Brown I used to be and he could find me something permanent."

However, back at Sutton Hoo, the priority in the weeks following the removal of the treasure and departure of the other archaeologists, was preserving the excavated imprint of the ship burial. There are several references in his letters at this time to the view of Mrs Pretty and her spiritualist friends that the war will be over in a matter of days or months. Basil, however, was taking no chances, writing to his wife: "I'm preparing the boat protection to last a year." With no regular job to return to, Mrs Pretty found work for Basil on her estate for a couple of weeks until finally he returned to Rickinghall on Saturday 16 September. The following Monday, Basil returned to Stanton Chare to continue where he had left off the previous year. The Ipswich Museum continued to pay him for his time on this dig until this was complete. Meanwhile, Basil was on the lookout for other paid employment.

A wartime role
A year before Basil's first excavations for Mrs Pretty at Sutton Hoo, he had become a Special Constable. The primary responsibility for such volunteers was to prevent riots and other breaches of the peace in their community. Basil's warrant card also gives instructions to be on the lookout for any person attempting to destroy road and rail bridges, as well as anyone seeking to interfere with telephone lines, sources of water and energy supplies.[2] On returning home to Rickinghall, Basil resumed this role as Special Constable, which was unpaid apart from payment of out-of-pocket expenses.

One of the specific duties he did perform in his role as Special Constable was the compilation of the local entries for the 1939 Register of the population of England and Wales which was compiled in late September. In the register, Basil describes his occupation as "Archaeologist - Foreman" and he records that he was an Air Raid Precaution (ARP) Warden.[3] This was a purely voluntary role, and his main duty was to ensure that no lights were visible from houses and businesses at night which might help enemy aircraft identify targets. ARP Warden Basil Brown would have been easily identifiable by his tin hat emblazoned with a large letter "W". Wardens were also required to report on the extent of any local bomb damage and to assess the local need for help from the emergency and rescue services. Fortunately, there was little of this work to be done in Rickinghall.

Basil Brown – undated but probably mid-1940s (Courtesy of Peter Christie)

In the witness box
It was whilst cycling back one day from his work at Stanton Chare, that Basil witnessed a violent assault which led to him being called to give testimony in court. On Friday 19 January 1940, the Ixworth magistrates heard the case of wounding by Ernest Whistlecraft, a labourer - and notorious poacher - from Rickinghall, against Robert Wallace a gamekeeper from Hinderclay. Mr Wallace gave his evidence from a stretcher placed near the witness box, having been in hospital since the assault on 1 December the previous year.

Basil described in court how he was cycling home from Stanton at about 4.30 in the afternoon on the day in question. When he reached the bottom of Snape Hill two boys called out to him. Brown continued:
"As I thought there had been an accident I went up the hill rather quickly and saw a man on the side of the road about twenty yards ahead, apparently jumping or dancing about. He had something in his hand, which I took to be a gun, but I wasn't sure because it was dusk. As I got near he jumped off the road into the gateway leading into the plantation and it seemed that as he did so he hit at something on the ground. I thought something was wrong, and called out 'Stop it!' at the same [time] throwing my bicycle on the side of the road."

Whistlecraft pleaded not guilty, and because of the serious nature of the crime, he was committed for trial at the Suffolk Assizes in Ipswich. A week later, Mr Justice Charles sentenced Ernest Whistlecraft to twelve months labour for what he described as a violent, brutal and entirely unprovoked attack on Wallace.[4]

The *Bury Free Press* also carried this short little cameo from the trial:[5]
Difference a Comma Can Make!
Only a small, insignificant comma, but its absence from a typescript which was supplied to Mr. Justice Charles at the Suffolk Assize on Friday elevated the standing of a witness to a position which temporarily perplexed his Lordship, for suddenly he asked, "What is a superior archaeologist?" Mr. Gerald Howard, one of the two counsel appearing in the case saw the point, and he explained that "superior" was the second name of the village from which the witness came, and that actually the typescript should read: "Basil John Brown, Rickinghall Superior, Archaeologist." Mr. Justice Charles replied that

he was rather puzzled for a moment. "I wondered what an inferior archaeologist was" he added amid laughter.

Another Sutton Hoo dig?

It was not the only newspaper coverage Basil received that year. At the end of March 1940, the national newspapers reported that the archaeologist was planning to excavate one of the other Sutton Hoo mounds. Under the heading "Saxon queen's grave to be opened", Basil is quoted as saying:

> "We shall probably open the mound next to Redwald's *[sic]*. There are still nine mounds waiting to be excavated, but the one I have in mind may be the grave of Redwald's Queen, and in that case will probably contain great riches." [6]

There had been continued interest in Sutton Hoo since the beginning of the war. Both the British Museum and the Ipswich Museum held exhibitions on Sutton Hoo in early 1940.[7] In February of the same year, Charles Phillips, who was back at Selwyn College, Cambridge, lectured on the 1939 excavation findings to the Society of Antiquities, paying tribute to Basil's excavation skills.[8] Phillips also picked up on the newspaper reports of a possible further dig. He wrote to Basil on 27 March: "I see from the Telegraph this morning that something may be moving again at Sutton Hoo ere long. Does this mean that the Ipswich folk are going to open up some of the little fellows?" Sadly, we do not know how Basil replied, although a further letter to him from Charles Phillips two days later, suggests that Basil refuted the reports. Phillips wrote: "I am disgusted to hear that these scribblers have been up to their games again ... I do not think that you need worry about it and I am sure that Mrs. P. knows enough about the way these things work to understand."[9]

A further wartime job

In July 1940, Basil obtained a full-time position at the Navy, Army and Air Force Institutes (NAAFI) working out of its regional headquarters in Newmarket Road in Bury St Edmunds.[10] He was a counter hand, selling food and drink to servicemen. From a handful of surviving letters Basil wrote to May during this period of employment, we know that he probably stayed in or near Bury during the week, cycling or taking the bus home to Rickinghall at weekends.[11] According to Basil, his team was short-staffed and the job was not what he would have liked, writing "the washing up is a bigger thing than I've ever seen, all I could do was the best I could", adding "I will I hope get through somehow unless Hitler drops a bomb on us, but I'm too busy to think of anything." His letters suggest that he may have been provided accommodation at Culford - probably under canvas alongside soldiers camping there - which was not altogether satisfactory. Basil writes: "I am not sure am feeling O.K. the rough conditions have had no effect on me up to the present." However, the pay was good and so he stuck it out.

Even during his employment with the NAAFI, Basil still found every opportunity to dig. Martin Chilvers records that one of Basil's duties was to dig trenches in which to bury surplus food. Ever the archaeologist, he chose a trench next to a Roman road in Culford Park, so that he might uncover evidence of the road surface. Basil's job with the NAAFI was relatively short-lived, lasting until mid-November 1940. The Bury St Edmunds headquarters was closed and although he was offered a job in London, Basil declined because he wanted to stay close to home. After the war, Basil applied for the Defence Medal based on his NAAFI employment. His application was unsuccessful because the medal was only granted to civilian staff who were authorised to wear khaki uniform, which Basil had not been.[12]

Job seeking again

Basil was, once again, seeking paid work. He had enlisted the help of Revd H A Harris, Honorary Secretary of the Suffolk Institute of Archaeology and Rector of Thorndon near Eye. Harris wrote to him on 18 November 1940: "I am sorry that I have had no luck in finding a suitable job for you - I have tried the army, a shop, a pub and other similar places that might suit you but so many county businesses are marking time on a skeleton staff." Revd Harris shared Basil's love of stamp collecting, as well as a passion for archaeology and the two men were regular correspondents.[13] The clergyman continued to counsel Basil on employment matters for the next year, including encouraging the Browns' idea of running a small shop for general goods, saying that it "would make you your own master and at present pays well." Although Basil did not pursue this idea, there is a possibility that he and May might have supplemented their income, for some time, selling stationery supplies.[14]

Adoption?

It was about this time that Basil and May Brown were considering adopting a young boy. The couple's marriage had been childless but their fondness for children was obvious throughout their lives. In the run-up to the outbreak of the war, while Basil was still at Sutton Hoo, May had taken in a number of early evacuees, presumably from London. Although her letters to Basil suggest that this was a far from pleasurable experience ("… one of the girls is a demon and awful liar …"), this did not seem to have put them off the idea of adoption.[15] Basil once again turned to Revd Harris for guidance who advised against formal adoption, warning of the permanence of the arrangement should the child "turn out to be a mill stone about your neck". Instead, he suggests that the Browns might consider a more temporary arrangement, working with a society that would pay an allowance towards clothing costs.

Basil had also told Edith Pretty of their desire to adopt as, writing back to him in December 1939, she says: "It is very brave and very kind to consider adopting a boy of six. It is a great responsibility but if you and Mrs Brown are both fond of children he would no doubt bring great joy into your lives."[16] Basil and May did not, in the end, adopt but both enjoyed having children around them, warmly welcoming those who visited their house, as well as taking a close and enthusiastic interest in their young neighbours.

Culford and West Stow

In early 1941, Basil successfully applied for a job as stoker at Culford School near Bury St Edmunds, then an independent, Methodist boarding school for boys. It was a job he retained until 1943 or 1944. Basil lived in the school porter's lodgings, cycling home to Rickinghall for the weekend every fortnight. Whilst employed at Culford, Basil took every opportunity to dig, accompanied by enthusiastic boys from the school. In February 1941, when they were excavating, the park was machine-gunned by enemy aircraft and Basil and the lads had to shelter in woodland until it was safe to come out.[17]

In June 1941, Basil, accompanied by one of the Culford School masters and a number of boys, started to excavate a site on West Stow heath. Basil had examined this area the previous December and in his Culford School project, Martin Chilvers describes how Basil came to dig there. He records:

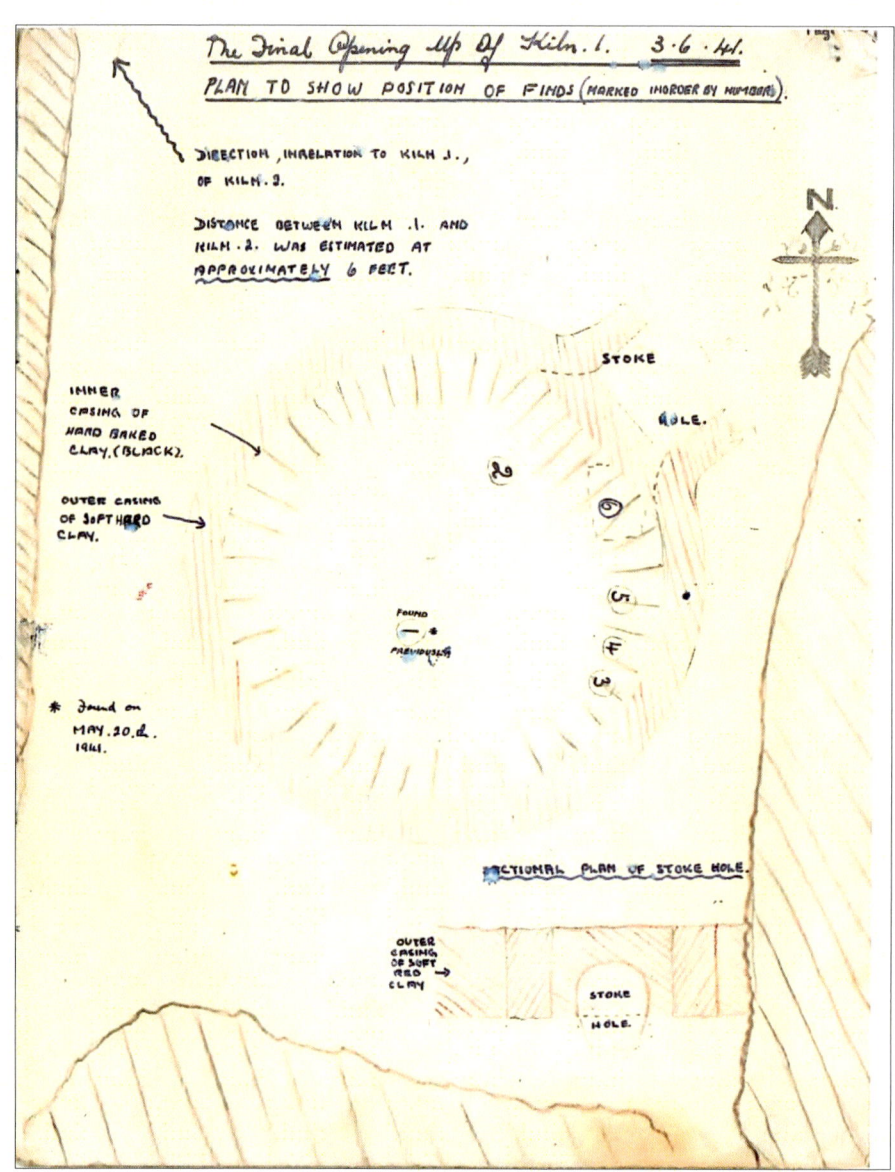

A page from Basil Brown Archive volume XXVI (SCCAS)

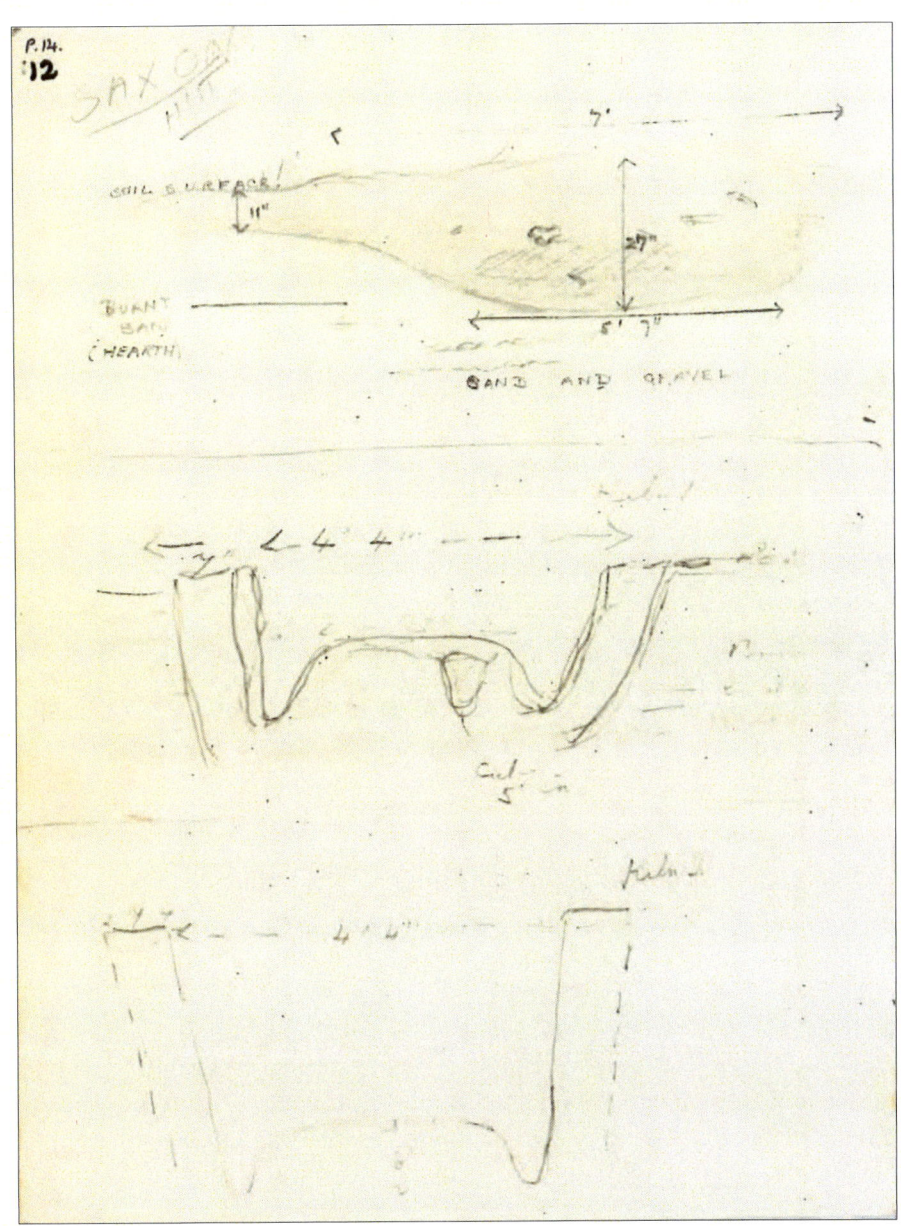

A page from Basil Brown Archive volume XXVI (SCCAS)

"Mr Brown found Roman pottery kilns during a look round the heath for evidence of Roman occupation during spare time from his Culford School work. He noticed the rising ground near the river as a likely site and he discussed it with the tenant Mr Thurston. The Forestry Commission owned the land. Mr Thurston's house was situated about three hundred feet from the two Roman pottery kilns he discovered later. Mr Thurston had been using the rising ground as a poultry run but kindly granted Mr Brown permission to look over the ground. Soon Mr Brown found sherds which were strewn about and when he scraped with a trowel he came across black earth."

Within days of the group's excavation in 1941, they had uncovered more pottery along with a first kiln. The discovery of a second kiln followed shortly after, together with more pottery and pig bones. Basil is also credited with the first discovery of signs of an Anglo-Saxon settlement at West Stow. His notebook recording his 1941 dig contains a sketch entitled "Saxon Hut" and shows a sunken feature building.[18]

Watching the skies
In September 1942, a Royal Observer Corps observation post was established at Micklewood Green, at the west end of Botesdale Common. Basil was one of a small band of civilian, volunteer observers who manned the post twenty-four hours a day, seven days a week, on a roster of four-hour shifts. The post consisted of a two-storey brick tower and an underground concrete bunker with basic accommodation. The team's task was to spot, track and report all aircraft so that the Home Defences could be warned of and act upon any threat of attack. The volunteers had to learn to recognise the different aircraft sounds and silhouettes.[19]

In November 1944, Basil passed the Intermediate Test of the Royal Observer Corps.[20] Andrew Dickson, who as a boy got to know Basil well recalls how Basil collected a large number of aircraft recognition manuals to help him in his role, as well as compiling a large scrapbook with cuttings on aircraft and the Royal Observer Corps. Andrew wrote of Basil: "He knew I was seriously interested in aeroplanes and always had been during my childhood so he probably felt I could provide a safe home for the whole collection. I still remember the excitement of going over to Rickinghall to collect everything and it is still all together and safe."

A page from Basil's wartime scrapbook (Courtesy of Andrew Dickson)

A page from Basil's wartime scrapbook (Courtesy of Andrew Dickson)

According to Martin Chilvers' school project, Basil's knowledge of the stars and of astronomy was welcomed by the team. One of Basil's fellow observers was Peggy Healey (née Fellingham). She recalled later in life that Basil Brown was known for his accurate weather forecasting. Peggy would often ask him what the weather was going to do, at which point he would hold his pipe in his hand and look carefully round at the sky before giving her his answer.[21]

In his element
At some point towards the end of the war, the museum employed him as an attendant at Christchurch Mansion in Ipswich. Dr Stanley West, who attributes his own successful career in archaeology to Basil, records: "I first got to know Basil in 1945 when I began to haunt the Ipswich Museum with bags of flint implements. [He] would talk archaeology with anyone who would listen."[22] Revd Ivan E Moore wrote in his memoirs: "Once he [Basil] showed me where he slept – in a large store cupboard with an ARP stretcher propped up on two packing cases for a bedstead. He was in his element."[23]

---

[1] Basil Brown Archive volume VII (SA/I: HD 3096/1/6).
[2] NT SH/BB2/PRIM/DOC/4h.
[3] TNA: RG101/6644D/002/1.
[4] Accounts of the trial appear in the *Bury Free Press* 20 January 1940, page 6 and *Bury Free Press* 27 January 1940, page 6.
[5] *Bury Free Press* 27 January 1940, page 5.
[6] *Daily Herald* 26 March 1940, page 12.
[7] Markham, 2002.
[8] *Halifax Evening Courier* 23 February 1940, page 7.
[9] These two original letters from Charles Phillips are to be found with the copy of Basil Brown Archive volume VII held by the SCCAS.
[10] His certificate of service is held by the NT (SH/BB2/PRIM/DOC/4i).
[11] Held by the SCCAS.
[12] NT SH/BB2/PRIM/DOC/4e.
[13] Several of Revd Harris' letters are to be found in Basil Brown Archive volume LXXXVIII (SCCAS).
[14] Basil wrote a list of various stationery items with prices inside the front cover of one of his notebooks - Basil Brown Archive volume IV (SA/I: HD 3096/1/13).

[15] May's (mainly undated) letters accompany the copy of Basil Brown Archive volume VII in the SCCAS.
[16] This original letter is to be found with the copy of Basil Brown Archive volume VII held by the SCCAS.
[17] Much of the information about Basil's time working at Culford has been gleaned from Martin Chilvers' school project. The date of the machine-gunning incident is given in Watson, 1980.
[18] Basil Brown Archive volume XXVI on loan from SCCAS to West Stow.
[19] Further information on the Botesdale Royal Observer Corps observation post can be found in Clayton, 2014.
[20] NT SH/BB2/PRIM/DOC/4g.
[21] From an interview in 2004 with Peggy Fellingham by her daughter and son-in-law, Marcia and Chris Bell.
[22] From a tribute to Basil Brown of 2007 and S West, 'A Life in Archaeology', *Proceedings of the Suffolk Institute of Archaeology and History* Vol XLIII, Part 3 (2015), pages 428-438.
[23] Held by Revd Moore's family.

Chapter 7
Peacetime

"Much interest was aroused in the village"

The end of the Second World War marked Basil Brown's return to work for the Ipswich Museum as an archaeological excavator. He also resumed his weekly reports to the museum which demonstrate the wide range of projects in which he was involved. For instance, in November 1945 Basil fieldwalked an area north of Pakenham windmill after a tip-off from Group Captain Livock, a fellow member of the Suffolk Institute Archaeology and Natural History. Livock showed Basil a sketch made by one of his Flight Lieutenants earlier in the year after having flown over the area. The airman had sketched what looked like a triple-ditch system surrounding a building. Basil confirmed the existence of the ditches and found that the area was covered with Roman pottery.[1]

A Roman villa
One of Basil's first major excavations for the museum after the war was at Castle Hill in Whitton on the outskirts of Ipswich. At the time of Basil's initial dig in the summer of 1946, the site was open fields and farmland. On Castle Hill meadow he found debris of Roman buildings and wall footings, as well as pottery sherds, broken roof tiles and a late 4th century coin. He returned in July 1948 before a housing estate covered the entire area, and opened further trenches which revealed evidence of two separate levels of Roman occupation. He uncovered a room with a hypocaust, as well as much coloured and decorated wall plaster and mosaic tiles. Numerous smaller finds were removed to the Ipswich Museum, including glass and bone games counters, a small bronze bow brooch and a silver rat tail spoon. Basil also found evidence of earlier Saxon and Late Iron Age or Neolithic occupation.[2]

According to Dr Stanley West, Basil dug at Whitton almost single-handedly and with the crudest of tools; Ipswich Museum's budget clearly didn't run to state-of-the-art equipment for their excavator. He recalls, however, run-ins between Basil and Harold Spencer at the museum, including over Basil's work at Castle Hill.[3] Revd Moore, who visited Basil on several of his digs, arrived at Whitton to find Basil with a mountain of earth by his side. Moore records: "Basil always maintained nothing was ever said at the time about his work at Castle Hill as he had dug so deep that the houses built on the site had to have extra foundations and there was a dispute between the Borough Housing and Museum Committees as to whose funds should meet the cost."[4]

A Botesdale kiln
Basil was by now a well-established local, "go-to" man if anybody ever uncovered something unusual. One of these many occasions was on 19 April 1946 which happened to be Good Friday. Perhaps Basil was settling down to a quiet weekend away from work? If he was, which is doubtful, then his plans were altered when: "Mr G Smith, Gardenhouse, Rickinghall reported that Roman pottery and red clay had been found at Botesdale during building operations and that some of the soil from the site had been carted to his land and also dumped in the Gardenhouse Lane. I examined the dump and found evidence that the soil had come from the stokehole of a Roman pottery kiln. I then visited site and confirmed this."[5] After having told his Ipswich Museum boss, Guy Maynard, and then interviewed the building contractor, Basil obtained permission from the District Council's surveyor to excavate "provided I did not hold up the building operations."

Basil enlisted the help of two of his now regular helpers, John Blake and Kenneth Landymore, and his friend, Major Kilner at Ixworth, also found Anthony Rudd to assist. They started work the following day. One of Basil's many typed reports of his excavations picks up the story. It says:
"On Easter Sunday excavations were continued with the help of Anthony Rudd and the remains of the kiln which had been cut through by the workmen were investigated. We then found that although a considerable portion of kiln wall had been cut away the central stand was still intact." Basil completed his excavation in just two days and recorded: "The residents near helped in many ways including storage of tools etc and as much interest was aroused in the village the police co-operated."
He also noted that he had removed some pottery and remains of the kiln baking floor to his shed![6]

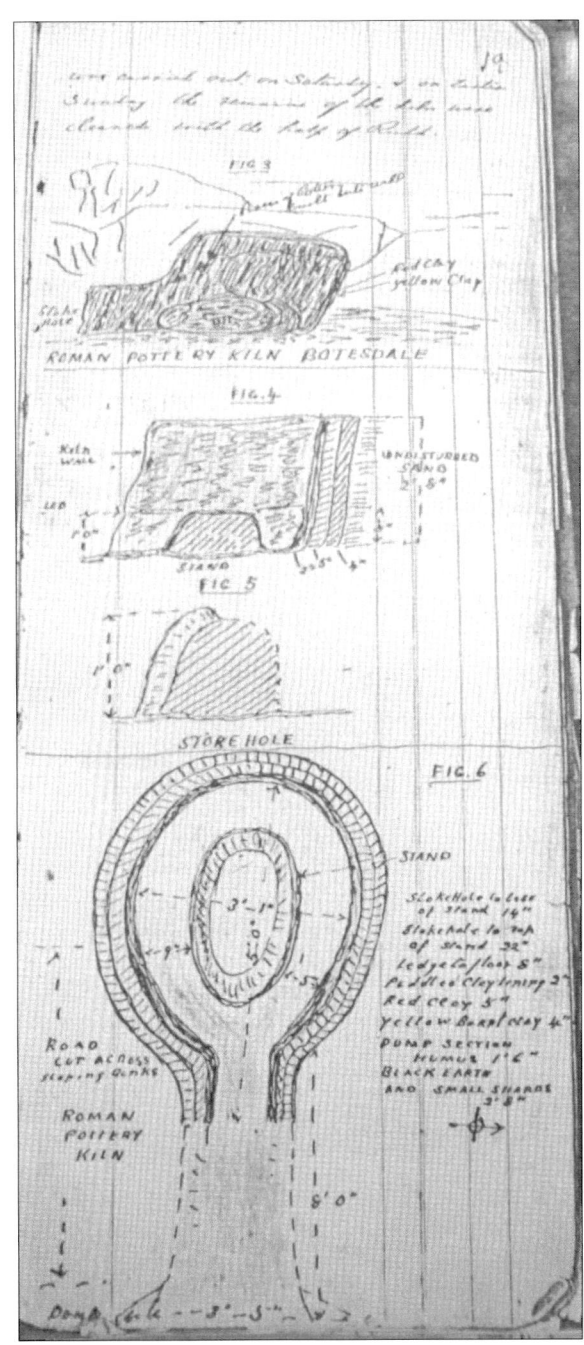

A page from Basil Brown Archive volume XCIII (SCCAS)

A Rickinghall kiln

It is perhaps not surprising, given Basil's drive to unearth all and everything in soil which may shed light on Suffolk's past, that he would even dig when on leave. Evidence of this is to be found in a report in the *Bury Free Press* which begins: "A Roman pottery kiln of unusual type has been discovered at Rickinghall by Mr Basil Brown, who is now a member of staff at Ipswich Museum, during his holiday. The find is interesting as adding another link in the chain of evidence which proves that the Wattisfield district was the chief pottery making centre in Suffolk during Roman times."[7]

A typed report by Basil, headed "Extension of Roman Settlement in Rickinghall" and dated 6 October 1946, gives details of his investigations:
"On Sept. 23rd 1946 I commenced excavations or rather a survey of the Roman site. Mr Smith allowed me to do what I liked on his Gardenhouse Field where only traces of Roman occupation had been found. The first find made after much calculation was a wall footing of grouted flints. This was found to belong to a building with a floor of beaten sand. This building was then partly excavated. It was then decided to test the surroundings and a trial to the S.E. revealed a small piece of kiln debris and the hole was enlarged and some red burnt clay was found. It was clearly the entrance to a Roman Kiln stokehole … Very few potsherds were found but these certainly belong to an early occupation. Close to the kiln was a Constantinian coin and later a small coin was found in the building, this apparently belonged to the reign of Gratian 175-183 AD."[8]

The newspaper article continues: "The pottery kiln bears some resemblance to one recently discovered during building operations in Botesdale, but it was larger, and its pedestal or central stand is better shaped. It was working about 1,700 years ago."

Return to West Stow

In 1947, Basil returned to West Stow and re-excavated the two Roman pottery kilns he had discovered in 1941. Dr Stanley West joined him on this dig and recalls that Basil "was totally dedicated to the study of archaeology and had a remarkable 'countryman's' feel for the landscape and soils. Above all he had a great joy in finding things, a fascination that he passed on to me and has never left me." West wrote of the excavation with Basil: "It was in the course of this work that it became evident that there was a spread of Early Anglo-Saxon potsherds in the rabbit-scrapes over the whole of the knoll and that sections of 'huts' could be seen in the small sand-pit in the north-east corner of the site."[9] Basil reportedly turned to Dr West and said something like: "I know what, I reckon this is where that Anglo-Saxon village was."[10]

Dr West went on to lead excavations at West Stow between 1965 and 1972, uncovering one of the most important early Anglo-Saxon settlements sites in England. His experimental work reconstructing Anglo-Saxon buildings ultimately gave rise to the recreated Anglo-Saxon village, museum and visitor centre there today. Basil continued to visit the site into the early 1970s.[11]

Saxon Rendlesham
One of the leading academic archaeologists who held Basil Brown in high regard was Rupert Bruce-Mitford who, as Assistant Keeper at the Department of British & Medieval Antiquities at the British Museum, was responsible for the Sutton Hoo treasures. It is clear from surviving letters to Basil from Bruce-Mitford, that the two men kept in regular touch. Among Basil's papers is a 1948 reprint of Rupert Bruce-Mitford's article on Saxon Rendlesham from the *Proceedings of the Suffolk Institute of Archaeology and Natural History*. It is annotated on the front "With many thanks for your help and advice – R B-M" and is dated February 1950.[12] The help and advice from Basil he refers to is the work Basil had undertaken for him the previous year.

In January 1949, Rupert Bruce-Mitford wrote to Basil saying: "You may perhaps have heard that I succeeded in locating a 6th century Saxon cremation cemetery in Rendlesham, at Hoo Hill. But there is something which looks like an archaeological site immediately to the south of the village school on the Green. I may perhaps later on ask you to dig a ditch and trench here, if you can find the time to do it." Then on 12 June, Bruce-Mitford penned a further letter to Basil in which he said: "I would very much like you to make a beginning with the trial trenches on Thursday June 16th, that is the day before I arrive at the site – if Mr Maynard agrees."[13] He also asks Basil to bring a few helpers if he can find some. Basil duly obliged although no pottery or artefacts were found.

Basil at West Stow in 1947 (SCCAS)

Basil watches Dr Stanley West excavating at West Stow in 1947 (SCCAS)

Return to Sutton Hoo

On 21 and 22 July 1949, Basil recorded in his notebook: "Received instructions from Mr Cullum and Mr Maynard to go to Sutton Hoo as the Electric Supply Company, Woodbridge Area, were putting in posts in the vicinity of the Sutton Hoo site." He noted that the line of the posts was east-west and went within about 150 yards of the mounds. He examined the area around each of the post holes and concluded: "The indications show that a channel had existed here. On the hill near, flints were found implying the possibility of a floor. To the south of the house, Sutton Haugh farm, are indications of a suitable landing place for ships which had once existed with the probable track to the mounds." Basil also took the opportunity to search the area surrounding the mounds where he found portions of two clench nails and one sherd of beaker pottery.[14]

Basil often found an opportunity to return to Sutton Hoo. In 1950 he recorded a visit in May with a Dr B Neuman who was interested in the small mounds which had counterparts in Sweden.[15] In 1952, Basil revisited the site, accompanied by Guy Maynard, where the pair spoke to visiting members of the Ipswich Historical Society, describing their methods of work at the 1939 excavation.[16]

Seeking answers

Sometimes, try as he might, historical conundrums remained unsolved, despite Basil's best efforts. In March 1951, the *East Anglian Magazine* printed this letter from Basil, accompanied by a photograph:

"This stone is in the corner of Rickinghall Inferior churchyard but it has no authentic history. Tradition says it is an ancient font which was removed from the church many years ago. Another version is that it was used for washing money at the time of the Plague. It may have been the base of a cross. No exact parallel is known but it apparently belongs to the Norman period, 1066-1189. Perhaps some of your readers may be able to supply an answer?"

Sadly, nobody seems to have come forward with their theories. It was one of the unexplained items Basil had clearly puzzled over for many years. Back in 1935, he had been photographed in the churchyard with the stone for a national newspaper with the accompanying caption: "Mr Basil Brown beside a curious old stone tank which he helped to unearth from the churchyard at Rickinghall. He believes it to be of Norman origin."[17]

Present-day historians remain baffled as to the stone's original use and it now sits outside the church porch and is filled with flowering plants. Jean Sheehan writes: "A description of it before the plants were added said that it bears traces of having been lined with lead and has sockets where it apparently fitted on to a plinth."[18]

Return to Cork Wood
It was in June 1951 that Basil returned to the scene of his first major successful dig. On and off, he dug there until December, and then again between July and December 1952. Basil's detailed weekly reports to the Ipswich Museum not only outline the work undertaken but also show how he managed get a wide range of people involved in this excavation in some capacity or other.

His report for the week ending 25 August 1951 starts: "During this week very good progress has been made at the Cork Wood site and the helpers have been very useful. Messrs Watsons employee has cut back the weedland growth above and near the remains, removed the stumps and roots and top soil. I have also had the vicar of St Matthews, Leicester who has been associated with Iron Age digs including Maiden Castle and has had much experience. Two schoolboys one from Culford School and the other from King Edward Grammar School have completed the team." This report and later ones record that Frederick "Jack" Watson frequently assisted Basil when not running his pottery business, and also provided tools for the dig.

The focus of Basil's excavations this time was on a pit shaft he had uncovered previously. In September 1952, the local newspaper carried a report entitled "New discoveries 4,000 years old" and describes how Basil and his team of helpers had discovered signs of a prehistoric camp: "Dark markings in the modern pit face were noticed a few years ago by Mr Basil Brown, the well-known archaeologist. Now excavations have revealed the layout of a lined shaft with puzzling features and is considered unique. Fragments of Beaker pottery (Early Bronze Age) and a large number of flint tools and lumps of clay were found in the lining. Remains of hutments

Experimental kiln firing in 1954

Basil with a replica kiln in Calke Wood (Courtesy of Peter Christie)

[encampments of huts] have been found nearby and in one of the drainage ditches pottery, a lance head or fish spear and the tip of a bronze spear have been recovered."[19]

Gilbert Burroughs, who got to know Basil at this time, recalled: "What surprised me is how he knew things were there. I was with him once at a small dig at what they call Foxledge Common at Wattisfield. It was just a bank with fern on it, he'd started to dig there, and he eventually found the site of some dwelling. How did he know it was there? I remember it plainly; there were big round flintstones and in the centre there was a dark part and he said, 'that's where the post was' and he prodded away, 'and these flintstones were to hold the posts up'. Even then I couldn't imagine how he knew it was there."

A time machine in Rickinghall and Wattisfield
In the autumn of 1953, Mr R M Cook of the Museum of Classical Archaeology in Cambridge, together with other experts from the Cambridge Laboratory of Geophysics, visited Basil's Foxledge Common and newly re-opened Gardenhouse Lane Roman kilns, armed with new technology which the *Bury Free Press* described as a "time machine".[20] The newspaper describes a "newly-designed 'dating' instrument which uses radioactive properties."

Several other newspapers carried the story explaining that "the basis of this inquiry is that the magnetic north continually changes its position and that the particles containing iron minerals in clay are magnetic. When the clay is heated sufficiently and then cooled the particles first swing towards the magnetic north and their position becomes fixed. So it is possible, in theory, to discover where the magnetic north was when the clay was last cooled."[21]

Experimental kiln firing
Not content with uncovering ancient kilns, Basil was curious to know the precise method by which the Romans fired their pots using the local clay. In his report dated 16 November 1952, to his superiors in Ipswich, he records: "The replica of a Romano-British pottery kiln in the wood is to be tried out with experimental pottery early in the week by Mr Watson." In fact, over the following six years, Basil and Jack Watson undertook numerous

experimental kiln firings to try to replicate the Roman pots which had been unearthed there.

Basil recorded of firings at Cork Wood in July 1955: "Obtained 3 pots for firing from Mr Watson. A hearth or kiln was then made as follows (and fired for 2-3 hours). In the hollow on shallow gravel pit where the firing pit of the replica kiln was made and used for experiments, the result was black pottery but not fired enough to stand water. A second firing was made on Tuesday but firing at start was too fierce and pots flaked."[22]

During some of the last firings, in 1958, Gilbert Burroughs (who married Jack Watson's daughter) was given the job of stoking the kiln and credits this experience with his lifelong interest in reproduction Roman pottery. He recalled of the experiments: "Basil and he [Jack Watson], having found all this mass of grey pottery in Foxledge Common were wondering why it was grey? Father-in-law was making thousands of flowerpots and they were all firing red with the same clay, and they were intrigued to know why? So, they thought they would experiment to find out how the Romans were making the same clay come out grey in colour. So, they built these kilns and they did a whole series of them. They fired the first ones in the same manner in an oxygen free kiln and they came out red, just the same as the flowerpots. By closing the kiln up, and reducing the atmosphere in the kiln, that changed the ferric oxide in the clay and they become grey pots."

Another holiday dig
In between his revisits to Calke Wood and Foxledge Common over a period of seven years, Basil found plenty of other local sites to investigate; often, like his Rickinghall and Botesdale kiln excavations, in his time off from working for the Ipswich Museum. In early 1952, Basil undertook a dig in a location close to his heart, where he had laid his parents to rest some decades previously.

---

[1] Details taken from Suffolk Heritage Explorer (https://heritage.suffolk.gov.uk/).
[2] Ibid.
[3] From a tribute to Basil Brown written by Dr West in 2007.
[4] From Revd Moore's memoirs, held by his family.
[5] Basil Brown Archive volume VIII (SA/I: HD 3096/1/1).

[6] This report is held privately.
[7] *Bury Free Press* 11 October 1946, page 5.
[8] In private hands.
[9] S West, 'A Life in Archaeology', *Proceedings of the Suffolk Institute of Archaeology and History* Vol XLIII, Part 3 (2015), pages 428-438.
[10] *East Anglian Daily Times* 13 February 2021
[11] Basil's yearly diaries record these visits and are at SA/I: Acc No 18855.
[12] This pamphlet is held by the SCCAS in Basil Brown Archive volume LXXXVII.
[13] These two letters accompany the pamphlet in Basil Brown Archive volume LXXXVII.
[14] Basil Brown Archive volume XIII (SA/I: HD 3096/1/7).
[15] Ibid.
[16] A press cutting from the *Evening Star* of 1 July 1952 is in Basil Brown Archive volume XIII (SA/I: HD 3096/1/7).
[17] This article from the *Daily Sketch* of 16 January 1935 was kept by Basil and is now held by the SCCAS.
[18] Sheehan, 2013.
[19] *Bury Free Press* 19 September 1952, page 9.
[20] Bury Free Press 4 September 1953, page 1.
[21] Press cuttings from the *Norfolk News* and the *Norfolk and Suffolk Journal and Diss Express* The reports which use identical wording are pasted into Basil Brown Archive volume IV (SA/I: HD 3096/1/13). The same volume has a handwritten note – written in a hand other than Basil's – with the same text. It suggests that Basil himself (or more likely his wife) fed these articles to the press.
[22] Basil Brown Archive volume IV (SA/I: HD 3096/1/13).

Chapter 8
The Brown School of Archaeology

"I do have an awful job getting money from them"

A Lady Chapel

In March 1952, Basil Brown started digging in the churchyard at Rickinghall Superior. He recorded how the project came about:

"Excavations on site of a chapel at St Mary's Church Rickinghall. These were considered during a talk with Mrs S P Flowerdew at the time she was collecting information for her proposed booklet on the parishes of Rickinghall Superior and Inferior, where the question came up as to the chapel believed to have existed, and very little reliable information concerning it was then available, and most of this was included in the notes collected by the late Rev Edmund Farrer FSA on the church and in which he gives the date of the porch as 1480-1500 and that of the nave about 1480 while an earlier date is given for the chancel, i.e. 1350. The western tower is dated about 1360-1400."[1]

Basil and his adult helpers, Mrs Flowerdew's husband and a Mr Townshend, soon made progress and on 12 March: "discovered wall foundations of a small building. This agreed with conclusions that the chapel would be outside the church and not within the nave as generally thought." The same day, they also found fragments of fifteenth-century stained glass, the best of which Basil sketched into his notebook.

Further work continued over the next couple of weeks. The local newspapers take up the story, the *East Anglian Daily Times* telling us that the "excavations have been carried out by Mr Basil Brown of Rickinghall by way of a 'holiday task'."[2] The *Diss Express* describes the background and the finds:

"A guild of Our Lady is mentioned in 1494 as existing in the parish of Rickinghall Superior and in the 16th century (1526) Thomas Sheppard gave to the Lady's Chappell of Rickyngale the Over, a donation of six and seven-pence, a goodly sum in those days. After this nothing further is known, the rubbing of a brass from the tomb of William Hovell who died in 1492 is recorded as being in the British Museum and the tomb itself was believed to have been destroyed when the church was restored in

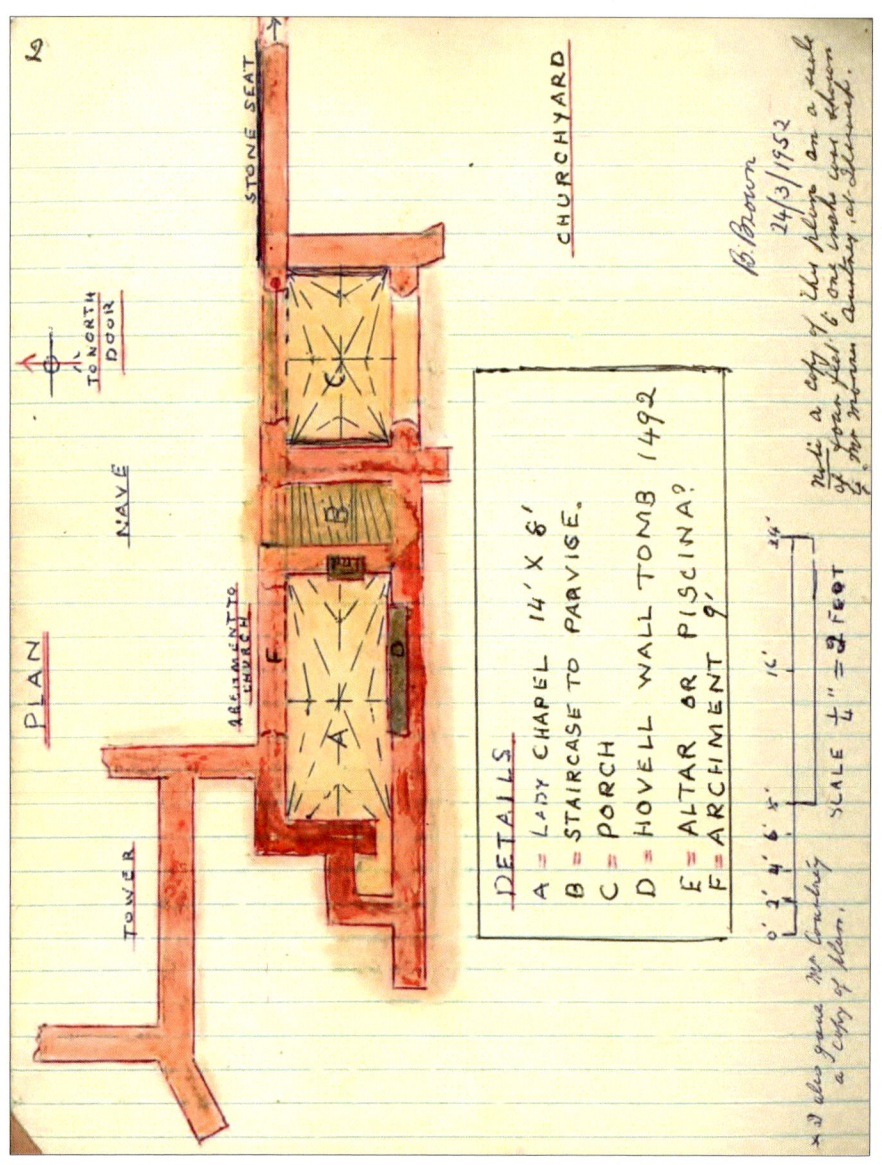

A page from Basil Brown Archive unnumbered notebook (SCCAS)

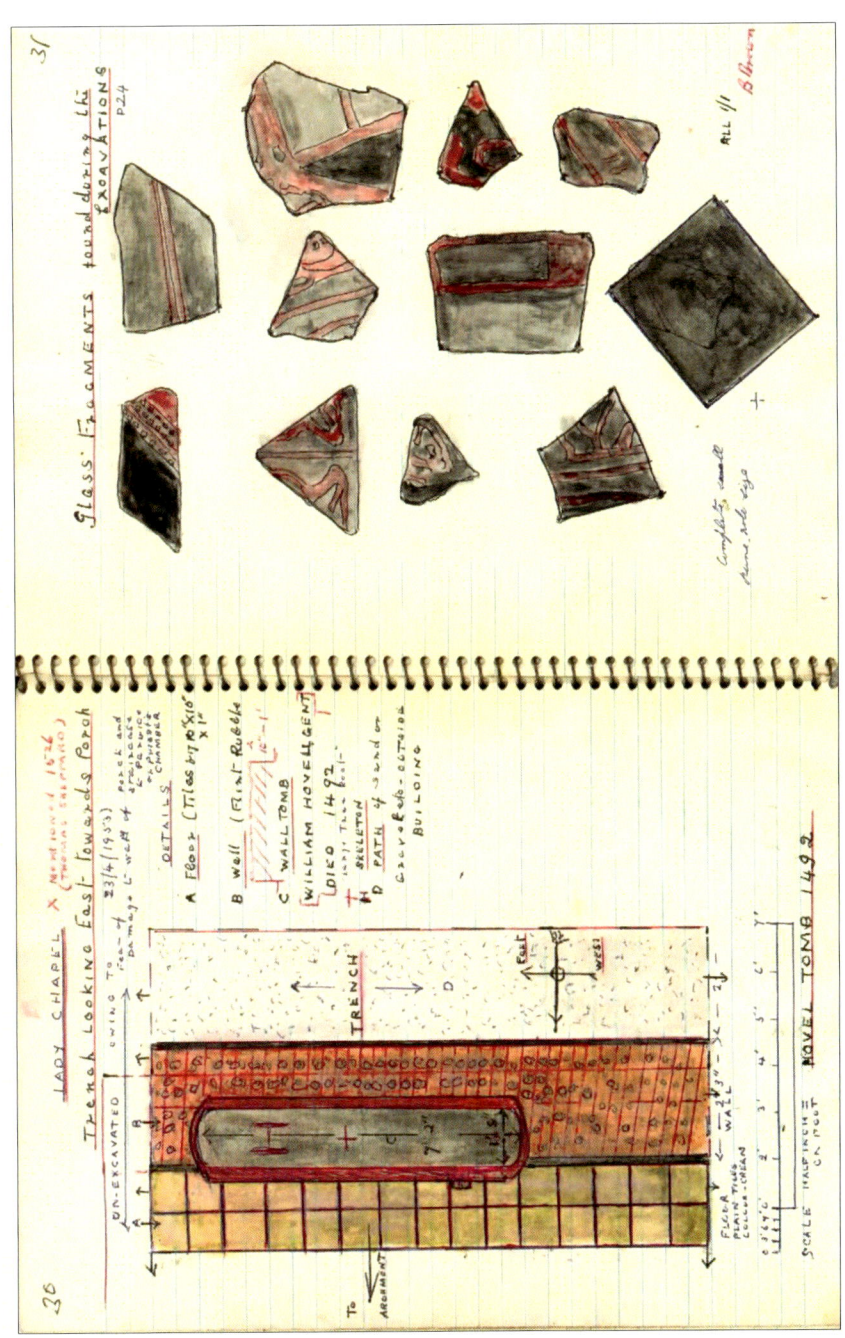

A page from Basil Brown Archive unnumbered notebook (SCCAS)

the middle of the last century. He was a member of the famous family of that name. A blocked archment in the church suggested that the chapel (and tomb) was within the nave but substantial foundations and the floor of a small building outside the church have been cleared, with the remains of the Hovell tomb. The floor tiles are in a good state of preservation, carved stones from the roof (of the Perpendicular period) have been discovered and fragments of encaustic or glazed tiles apparently from the altar which appears to have been built in the wall to the east. The building is 14 feet by 8 with a porchment on the west and with the existent south porch of the church and staircase to the parvise or priest's chamber formed an associated block."[3]

The local church authorities were no doubt pleased with Basil's discoveries which shed further light on the history of St Mary's Rickinghall Superior. However, a hint of frustration with Basil's holes can perhaps be discerned in a short, handwritten letter sent to him on 8 April 1953 by R Holt-Wilson, the Honorary Secretary and Treasurer, which reads: "The Churchyard Committee have instructed me to write and ask whether you would arrange to have the excavations at the upper church filled in by Whitsun, please?" In fact, Basil had already started this job a few days previously and he recorded on 23 April: "The ground was levelled and work completed about 12.30pm (S[ummer] T[ime])."[4] Basil had complied with instructions, in fact completing the job a full month ahead of the deadline.

A difficult relationship

In between his "holiday tasks" Basil continued his work as an excavator for the Ipswich Museum. Guy Maynard, with whom Basil had maintained a close and respectful relationship, retired from his job as Curator in 1952. The following year, Norman Smedley took over and Basil immediately found himself at odds with his new boss. He had been detailed to investigate a site in the parish of Pakenham near Ixworth, and Basil had begun digging in the spring of 1953. On 10 July, the *Bury Free Press* carried a short piece under the heading "How those Romans loved oysters!" which reported that: "Interesting archaeological discoveries have been made at Grimstone End, Pakenham. In the course of excavating for sand and gravel a Roman pottery was discovered. Mr Basil Brown, the archaeologist, then took charge and proceeded to make further excavations, during which he has unearthed what is considered to be an Anglo-Saxon pottery." The article describes Basil's finds which included two benches upon which pottery was fired, over sixty circular clay weights ("used, it is thought, for an Anglo-Saxon loom"), a bracelet and bone comb dating from the same era, as well as animal bones and oyster shells.

It was only a matter of days later, that a letter from Mr Smedley was posted through Basil's letterbox. In it, Smedley wrote: "I was very greatly disturbed to read an account of the find in the local paper. I do not, of course, know whether you gave any information to the Press, but I thought that I had made it clear that I favour a very careful handling of anything of the sort. A great deal of damage can be done as the result of premature publicity, and in future any request for information should be passed on to me." It is a further paragraph which perhaps gets to the heart of Norman Smedley's concerns. It reads: "The account was also misleading, as it gave the impression that this museum had only visited the site, and not that we were responsible for any archaeological investigations."[5]

These differences were, apparently, set aside and work continued at Pakenham with Basil, perhaps, under a slightly tighter rein. One local resident who, as a boy and young man, knew Basil commented: "It was very seldom that Basil complained, but on one of those occasions it was about the Ipswich Museum. They were very, very reluctant to reimburse him for bus fares and things like that. He said 'I don't go on long journeys. It's not much, but I do have an awful job getting money from them'."

A kindly face
For many children growing up in Rickinghall and Botesdale, Mrs Brown was more in evidence as a local character than Basil. This was partly because of May's role as a local press reporter and also because she went to church. Sally Green (née Davey), who spent six years as a choirgirl, recalled: "Mrs Brown would always sit on the back pew to the right just inside the door. She had a very distinctive voice and a kindly face. She always wore a cloche type hat and quite short skirts for the time. Her clothes were sombre but her aprons prettier." Derek Lummas grew up in the house next door to the Browns. As the eldest child, he spent a lot of time with Basil and his wife: "May used to treat me like a son and I used to keep rabbits, a pet jackdaw and pigeons. I also had two tortoises and a dog. May used to like to help me with the rabbits."

May Brown (Courtesy of Derek Lummas)

There is no doubt that May was a devoted wife and loved Basil dearly. One person remarked: "I remember my mother talking about Mrs Brown. What a saint she was as Basil had so often been away digging." However, May was fiercely proud of her husband's achievements. Those locals who knew the Browns have commented that it was May, rather than Basil, who often spoke up about Basil having been sidelined at Sutton Hoo and how he was not paid enough by the Ipswich Museum. One other local resident commented that: "Basil was terribly unworldly where money was concerned, because it didn't mean a thing to him." For some, May cut a rather fearsome figure and one of the Brown's neighbours recalled: "I remember seeing her advancing towards the house and she appeared to move in an almost tank-like manner, as though she didn't have legs, but on wheels. So, I suspect that she wasn't the sort of lady you would argue with."

Searching in the rubble
Although Basil's real gift was for digging beneath the ground, he also relished the opportunity to research local history through the buildings and surviving documents. In early 1953, he spent some time on the site of the former Redgrave Hall. The Lord of the Manor, John Holt Wilson, had taken the difficult decision to demolish the house to raise money to keep the estate as a whole running. All that remained were the kitchens – the core of the previous Tudor house around which the Georgian hall had been constructed – and the cellars beneath. Holt Wilson hoped to incorporate these into a new house at some time in the future (which sadly never happened). Basil made sketches of the crumbling remains, including the doorway with the Bacon crest over the top. He also took a series of photographs of the remaining Tudor structure and another photo which is labelled "Stone from early house probably original as of Abbot Samson."[6]

Basil recorded his investigations into the damaged coat of arms above the main, south door of the Tudor hall to the Ipswich Museum in his weekly reports of 21 February and 1 March: "Mrs Wilson has loaned me photographs. I have much of its history and an explanation of details and the motto … I carefully removed all building debris from near the south door looked carefully through the material, and spread it so that a heavy rain would wash it free from lime mixture. In spite of the search no sign of fingers and trowel could be found … No other features or minute details

A page from Basil Brown Archive volume II (SCCAS)

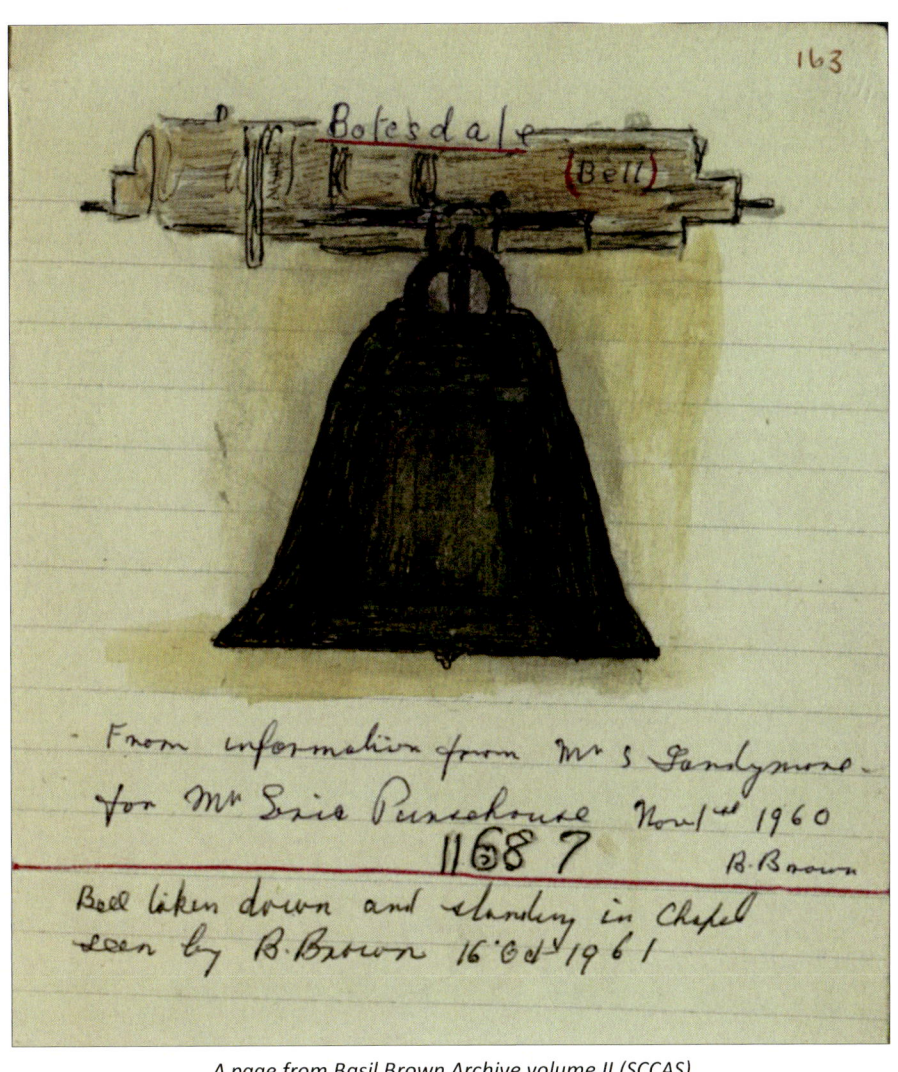

A page from Basil Brown Archive volume II (SCCAS)

which should appear on the stone are damaged as far as I could see by field glasses and the traces of gilt on the Latin motto of Sir Nic. Bacon shows plainly."[7]

The bell
Basil was consulted by other amateur historians, including Eric Pursehouse of Diss. Pursehouse was the son of a former headmaster at Redgrave School and wrote on the local history of Diss and the surrounding area. He was particularly interested in the Chapel of Ease and the adjoining property in Botesdale. This had once been a Grammar School founded by Sir Nicholas Bacon.

Basil Brown and Eric Pursehouse exchanged correspondence on the former school, especially the bell which, until 1961, sat atop the chapel building.[8] Basil consulted volumes in the Cullum Library in Bury Edmunds where he copied a drawing of the inscription on the bell. Along with a boar (the Bacon symbol), it gave the date 1687 and the name of the bellfounder, Thomas Doo.[9] He also consulted locals and drew the bell itself; at the time, still hanging in its original position.

A broken nose
An intriguing local history conundrum to which Basil returned several times was the carvings of heads at the top of three of the stone pillars in Rickinghall Inferior Church. Basil's sketches of the three faces - a king, a queen and an abbot or bishop - appear a few times in his notebooks.[10] Two sets are undated and another set was drawn by him in 1953. These 1953 sketches have, however, been pasted over by another set dated 10 November 1967. Basil notes that in 1956 the nose of the bishop/abbot was damaged.

Basil was convinced that the king and queen were accurate depictions of actual monarchs and set out to discover who they were. By comparing the crowns on his sketches with published pictures of monarchs, Basil concluded that they were Edward II and his wife, Queen Isabella. He notes that "Figures of Edward II and his queen are on the spandrels in roof of Burford Church Oxon. It may be well to confirm this."

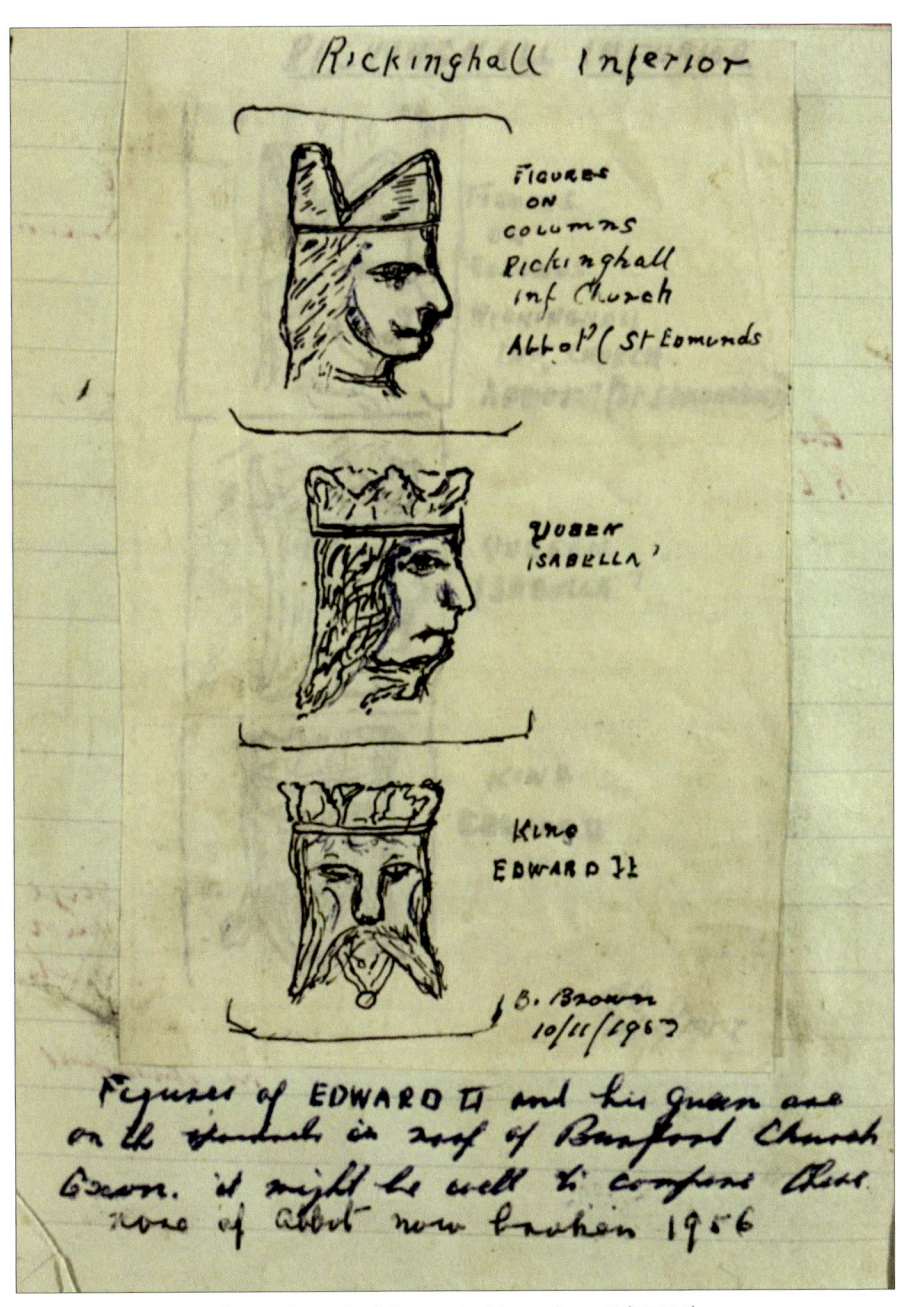

A page from Basil Brown Archive volume II (SCCAS)

A doorway emerges
It was not uncommon for Basil's name to crop up in local newspaper reports on finds under and above ground. Sometimes, of course, these were written by Basil himself and fed to the newspapers, often by his wife. At other times, he was described as the local archaeological or historical expert. For instance, in April 1961 a local paper reported a rare find made by a plasterer during renovations to the exterior of one of the oldest properties in Botesdale; a fourteenth-century house called St Catherine's.[11] The article describes how an old door arch with wooden dragon carvings had been uncovered and says that: "Mr Basil Brown, the local archaeologist, was immediately called in for consultations with the owner." Basil, of course, made detailed notes and sketches of the discovery.[12]

A return to Roman times
"There's no telling what the earth can yield", begins a newspaper report in the *Bury Free Press* of 26 March 1954. It continues: "Patches of different coloured soil can mean a lot to the experienced eye, and secrets of the past can be brought to light." In this case, the "experienced eye" was George Salter, of Brick Kiln Farm in Rickinghall, who decided to do some digging. It wasn't long before he found some old pottery which he took to "expert Basil Brown, well-known archaeologist, who pronounced them to be Roman."

Thus, began another of Basil's excavations on his doorstep, resulting in the discovery of a Roman pottery kiln, along with further pieces of pottery. The article concludes by saying: "Mr Brown told Ipswich Museum, for which he works, of the discovery and was helped with the excavations by the Curator, Mr N Smedley, and archaeologist Mr S West. Local schoolboys helped too."

Basil's helpers
All through his life, Basil was clearly a huge part of many residents' lives in Rickinghall and the surrounding area. He is variously described in recorded memories as friendly, unassuming and gentle. Basil is remembered locally, above everything else, for his constant willingness to make time for children, and to enthuse them about history and archaeology.

Indeed, Edgar Phillips, one of Basil's many correspondents, noted in a letter to the archaeologist in 1964 after a visit to see Basil Brown's last dig at Broom Hills in Rickinghall: "I was glad to note that you had a good complement of young helpers to assist you. The Brown School of Archaeology is already in being".[13]

In the early 1950s, there was a short-lived venture called the British Schools Archaeological Guild, and Basil Brown was invited onto the committee. It was established to encourage and foster interest in archaeology amongst schoolchildren. The first camp for schoolboys organised by the guild took place on the Sussex Downs, where they learned excavating techniques at a Romano-British site.[14] There is no evidence that Basil attended this event, although he was updated regularly on the organisation's progress.

Sadly, the guild ran into difficulties after a year or so and was finally disbanded in 1954.[15] But Basil's enthusiasm for nurturing the young's love of history continued. One local schoolchild recalled: "He was a lovely old gentleman who seemed to have two languages. He had one for intellectuals and adults and another one for children. He always seemed to speak to people in a language they could understand."

Digging for treasure
Basil's enthusiasm for digging up the past certainly rubbed off on his young next-door neighbour, Derek Lummas, who dug in his own back garden in the hope of finding buried treasure, which he ultimately did! In 1953, 12-year-old Derek unearthed an object which was significant enough for the local newspaper to report the find in its junior column, saying: "Recently, while digging in his father's back garden he discovered an old hand-painted scent bottle – colours as good as the day they were put on. It fascinated Derek, so, through the help of a neighbour, a china expert was consulted. Result? The expert dated it back to 1700 and pronounced it to be English Delft ware."[16] The article continues by explaining that unfortunately the neck of the bottle was broken and the stopper missing, but that if it were complete, it would be worth £50. "So, Derek is going to look for the stopper – but not this year because a crop of onions now flourish where the bottle was found!".

Pages from Basil Brown Archive volume II (SCCAS)

Spurred on by this interesting find, Derek continued to dig and in April 1955, he carefully excavated another patch in his garden. Nearly 3 feet beneath the level of the grass, Derek uncovered a Roman serpent brooch. Alongside a sketch of the brooch, a drawing of the hole's cross section with the brooch's location marked with an "x", as well as a photograph of the site, are the following comments made by Basil in his notebook: "Bought by B Brown for 10/- April 1st 1955. On loan to the British Museum."[17]

It is highly likely that the find was not worth as much as Basil paid Derek for it. If so, it demonstrates Basil's eagerness to enthuse and motivate the young to continue to delve into the past.

False teeth and an old bicycle.
All those who knew Basil in later life remembered his false teeth and his old bicycle. Andrew Dickson recalled: "Crumpled tweed jacket, flat cap, and small round glasses, false teeth that clattered as they tried to keep up with his animated jaw, old bicycle and the satchel with notebooks. Enthusiasm, energy and natural gift for a special science, tempered with modesty. That was the Basil Brown I knew." Derek Lummas remembered that they all thought it amazing how Basil had cycled all the way to Sutton Hoo and back, as well as everywhere in between. He marvelled at how someone not well built – although not frail either – without an ounce of fat on him, could cycle so much on a bike with no gears.

Another wonderful memory we have from another man who grew up in the village is this one: "I can't disassociate Basil from his bicycle. It was almost part of his anatomy. And I never knew a man who could cycle so slowly without falling off. You'd see him coming up the hill and think, he's got to fall off sometime. We were just coming back from the Coop, when Basil passed us on his bicycle very, very slowly. And as he got level with us, he coughed. And ejected his teeth straight into the road. Basil was, in one sense, almost an oddity in the village but he was respected. As kids, you could make someone's life a misery, couldn't you? There was a policeman in the village - we made his life a misery! But I never heard anybody say a bad word about Basil, or tease him, or laugh at him. He was a treasure."

A fascinating museum
The Brown's home in Rickinghall, Cambria, was a modest end of terrace house. Gilbert Burroughs recalled: "Like anyone who met Basil you were intrigued by his home even in those days. I mean it was not the sort of home that you had perhaps been used to. All his bits and pieces were everywhere, and you got the impression that May, his wife, was very frustrated by having all this junk, as she used to call it, in her house, although he did seem to keep it in one part of the house particularly, where the old range was with all his books."

Graham Clayton, who also visited Basil at home, recorded: "I do very clearly remember the front room, which I think on at least three of the four walls were solid bookcases, stacked floor to ceiling with books, for which he apologised as a lot of the books were also piled on the floor, since clearly there wasn't enough space. This apparently upset his wife, whom he said was not interested in history. He made that very clear."

To a boy like Andrew Dickson: "The house was like a fascinating museum to us. Small rooms full of interesting things. Such a variety, each with its own story. Among the objects was a mummified cat's head, apparently from a shipment of mummified cats brought to Liverpool in the 1800s from Egypt." This story was verified by Peter Christie who was given this object by May after Basil's death. He wrote:
> "[It] was a small, glass-fronted box containing a shapeless, black lump. Closer inspection revealed the weave of some fabric and a bone where the material had been cut across. I wouldn't have known what to make of this but for a flaking and fading newspaper cutting (undated) stuck to the back of the box."[18]

This cutting tells of the arrival in Liverpool of a consignment of 180,000 embalmed cats believed to have been buried in around 2,000 BC.

Derek Lummas remembered Basil having a large globe: "Instead of the earth as we know it when you look at it with countries on, he had it with stars on." Other schoolchildren who visited him also remember Basil's beautifully presented stamp collection, including a volume of Penny Blacks and another of Twopenny Blues.

This photo of Basil appeared in the Bury Free Press in 1966 (Courtesy of Iliffe Media)

One local schoolgirl, Sally Green (née Davey), asked for Basil's help with a school project. He obliged by putting a collection of archaeological finds together for her. This is what she remembers of the occasion: "I was thrilled to bits but also a little apprehensive to fetch the collection by myself. I need not have worried. Mrs Brown said 'hello' and showed me into the room on the right of the front door. It was stuffed with papers and boxes and tins, and it smelt of sweet tobacco. Basil Brown sat in a chair to the right of the fireplace and carefully took the lid off the biscuit tin. The tin was full of pieces of pot and bone and metal. Basil Brown told me about each item. I have no idea how long I was there that evening, but the memory is pleasant and unhurried. The next day my classmates at school had the whole collection out during the history lesson. I just remember being very proud of this loaned collection and took it back to Basil Brown with a big 'thank you'."

A celebrity speaker
Basil was not only popular with the youngsters. He was also in demand as a speaker to local adult groups. In January 1952, Basil was invited to the Rickinghall Women's Institute meeting, at which 36 members were present. They were treated to a "stimulating and informative address by Mr Basil Brown on the 'History of Antiquities of Rickinghall'."[19] The following year, Mrs Flowerdew, who had given the vote of thanks to Basil at this meeting, published a booklet on the history of the two Rickinghall parishes (Superior and Inferior) entitled *Rickinghall in the County of Suffolk*, in which she acknowledged expert help from Basil, as well as drawing on his various archaeological finds. And when a new banner for the Rickinghall Women's Institute was created in 1954, it featured a Saxon woman called Britfelda who had farmed 200 acres in the village. Basil was, naturally, consulted by the group who checked the accuracy of the dress and other details.[20]

Further invitations for Basil to speak came in. In September 1955 he gave a talk on the history of Botesdale, showing some examples of various finds made in the area, to the Botesdale Women's Institute.[21] Then in December 1956, Basil spoke on local archaeological discoveries, as well as the Sutton Hoo ship burial, to members of the Botesdale Methodist Guild. His talk was illustrated by lantern slides.[22] [23] Basil kept press cuttings reporting many of his talks, which appear pasted into his notebooks.

Retirement

Basil's last official day working for the Ipswich Museum was on 2 September 1961. He was 73 years old. Perhaps not surprisingly, Basil had 21 days' untaken leave and was therefore paid for these days in lieu of holiday.[24] Because Basil had been employed on a casual basis for the duration of his work with the museum, he did not receive an occupational pension. Instead, he and May relied solely on the basic state pension.

In the last few months of his employment, Basil had excavated primarily back at Grimstone End – this time working on some Roman burials which had been discovered – and at Facon's Hall in Rickinghall. Again, unsurprisingly, Basil continued digging at Facon's Hall for several years after his retirement.

---

[1] Basil Brown Archive unnumbered notebook (SA/I: Acc No 18855) covers the entire Rickinghall Superior dig, as well as Basil's research notes on the parish, church and the Hovell family.
[2] This article is from the *East Anglian Daily Times* of 27 March 1953 is pasted into Basil Brown Archive unnumbered notebook (SA/I: Acc No 18855).
[3] *Diss Express* 28 March 1952, page 4.
[4] Basil Brown Archive volume II (SA/I: HD 3096/1/14).
[5] Mr Smedley's original letter is in Basil Brown Archive volume XIX (SA/I: HD 3096/1/16).
[6] Basil Brown Archive volume II (SA/I: HD 3096/1/14).
[7] Held by the SCCAS.
[8] Four of Eric Pursehouse's letters to Basil are held by the NT in SH/BB2/PRIM/DOC/13.
[9] Basil Brown Archive volume II (SA/I: HD 3096/1/14).
[10] Ibid. and Basil Brown Archive volume XI (SA/I: HD 3096/1/12).
[11] *Diss Express* 7 April 1961 page 3.
[12] Basil Brown Archive volume XXVIII ((SA/I: Acc No 18855).
[13] This is held by the SCCAS.
[14] *Illustrated London News* 2 May 1953, page 30.
[15] Both the SCCAS and NT hold letters to Basil from, and about, the guild.
[16] This press cutting from the *Bury Free Press* 14 May 1954, page 11 is pasted into Basil Brown Archive volume II (SA/I: HD 3096/1/14).
[17] Basil Brown Archive volume II (SA/I: HD 3096/1/14).

[18] Peter Christie wrote a letter on this artifact in the *Fortean Times* Issue No 50, Summer 1988.
[19] *Bury Free Press* 25 January 1952, page 6.
[20] *Bury Free Press* 10 September 1954, pages 7 & 8.
[21] *Bury Free Press* 23 September 1955, page 4.
[22] *Bury Free Press* 7 December 1956, page 9.
[23] Two boxes of lantern slides, as well as two further boxes of some 150 glass slides, are held in the Basil Brown Archive (SA/I: Acc No 18855). A notebook with a list of lantern slides is at Basil Brown Archive volume XXIX (SA/I: Acc No 18855).
[24] NT SH/BB2/PRIM/DOC/7t.

Chapter 9
Retirement

"In some cases, distortion of facts has arisen"

For many, retirement is a time to relax, put one's feet up and spend time pursuing interests for which, hitherto, there hasn't been time. Not so for Basil Brown. His digging went on without a pause. Basil was now able to excavate and investigate where he chose, with the landowner's permission, of course. He was also freed up from his weekly obligation to report on his activities to his employers. Although from 1961 onwards, Basil stayed closer to home, he had no shortage of places to research. He also remained an active member of the wider community: In 1964 he was nominated as a candidate for election as a Rickinghall Superior Parish Councillor.[1]

The largest manor excavation in the country

Basil spent the first few retirement years, on and off, digging at Facon's Hall (now called Falcon's Hall) in Rickinghall. This lengthy project was sparked by a discovery of a patch of red earth during clearance of an orchard to make way for a tennis court. It took a matter of hours of scouring the site before Basil declared that it appeared that a manor house, dating from the twelfth or thirteenth century, had once stood on the spot.[2] Later, he told a newspaper reporter that it was certainly the largest and about the only manor excavation in the country.[3]

Basil had begun the excavation in his final few months of employment and reported of the site: "This is of course the main manor of Rickinghall Superior and in pre-war days I studied a good deal of its history from documentary evidence. Later these were sold and purchased by Chicago and are in the USA."[4] [5] Indeed, several of his notebooks contain detailed research notes taken from a wide range of sources. During the summer of 1961, Basil regularly travelled into Bury St Edmunds on a Saturday where he often consulted the Archivist at the Record Office, Mr M Statham, or his assistant. He recorded information gleaned from these experts, as well as research from the various documents and books available in the archives on Angel Hill.

Basil at Facon's Hall in 1966 (Courtesy of Peter Christie)

During the Facon's Hall excavation, Basil uncovered the remains of no less than three properties, the oldest dating back to Saxon times. As ever, he had several helpers, one of which was schoolboy Paul Rayson who was pictured with Basil in an article in *The Journal* of 24 May 1963.[6] The report informed readers that Basil had found evidence of underground furnaces, as well as parts of an 18-foot-wide Norman moat. It also referred to the find of a fourteenth-century currycomb, a comb used for grooming horses. Another significant artefact at Facon's Hall was unearthed by another of Basil's helpers, Richard Carver of Pakenham. This was a Saxon, twisted bronze wire ring with a green stone which Basil suggested might even have been belonged to the Saxon woman, Britfelda.[7]

Financial assistance

Barely a couple of months after Basil's retirement, at a Council meeting of the Suffolk Institute of Archaeology, his former boss, Norman Smedley, raised the subject of Basil's financial situation. Smedley suggested that, in recognition of Basil's valuable archaeological fieldwork over a period of some decades, the institute might sponsor a Basil Brown Fund with the aim of providing Basil with a regular allowance to top up his state pension. The Council resolved to set up an appeal and it donated 50 Guineas to start the fund.[8]

The *Bury Free Press* of 15 December 1961 carried a letter from the President and the Financial Secretary of the Suffolk Institute of Archaeology, seeking donations from the wider public. In January 1962, Basil received his first monthly payment of £2 10s and these continued until the end of 1966 when the fund ran out of money.

A record of every find

From the copious notes Basil kept throughout his life, it is clear that he meticulously recorded each and every find both of his own and by others. At his old school in Rickinghall, Derek Kemp found a coin during building work and duly took it to Basil to identify. Basil records that it was a silver Groat dating from the late fourteenth century, adding that it was "bent, but a nice coin of period of interest in parish history."[9] He took and kept a rubbing of the coin, returning the original to Mr Kemp.

Just up the road, Mr F Willimott found a coin-like object in the garden of Snape Hill Lodge and, again, asked Basil for information on what it was. Basil kept a rubbing of the disc and noted that it was a seal matrix, used to make an impression on a wax seal to authenticate a document, dating from 1700.[10] It depicted on one side William III on his horse. On the reverse were the arms of the House of Nassau, together with a lion rampant and a depiction of Britannia. Some of these objects were, no doubt, kept by the finders. Others may well have made their way into Basil's sheds.

Busy in sheds
Peter Christie, who became a close friend of Basil's in the archaeologist's retirement, said of his visits to the Browns' house in Rickinghall: "Every visit to Cambria began the same way - a chat over the latest archaeological news, a cup of Camp coffee prepared by May and then either a walk to Basil's latest excavation or to his shed in the garden; a structure that looked as though it had grown organically bit by bit."

Arthur Bryant, too, commented that "Basil's shed was a sight to behold. It was made of old pieces of wood and tin, anything he could find. If a piece fell off, he just nailed on another patch." Andrew Dickson recalled a number of small sheds of which he said: "They were packed with all sorts of things retrieved from the countryside. Mainly ancient pottery but also fossils, bones, metal artefacts and so on. They lined the shelves apparently randomly, but he always knew exactly where everything was and what it was."

Basil's diaries dating from the 1960s and 1970s are simply littered with entries in which he describes days on end working in his sheds, even in January when it must have been perishingly cold. For instance, on Tuesday 23 January 1968, he records: "Busy in sheds and generally clearing up. Also completing the putting up of shelves etc. Also getting specimens and boxes in place in a more satisfactory order. More labelling is required etc but the general appearance in sheds is the best possible." Barely a week later, he notes: "Busy in sheds putting up shelves and rearranging boxes and specimens. Also worked over any weak places in roof or walls."[11]

Basil and his sheds in the back garden at Cambria (Courtesy of the Compton family)

Inside Basil's sheds (SCCAS)

Bones

Throughout Basil's archaeological career, he excavated literally thousands of artefacts. His notebooks often tell us when these objects were sent to the Ipswich Museum. There are also occasional lists of items handed to the museum, often finds made by others helping him on digs, or simply uncovering them. Lists of these objects also appear in Basil's notes, perhaps some having spent some time residing in his shed. These included the remains of a bronze bowl, an iron shield boss and a long sword in pieces from Ixworth Thorpe, specimens of broken quern and pit stones from a dig he had undertaken in Fakenham and the "Remains of skeleton found at Fakenham and excavated beneath hut floor and wire under chin."[12]

Back in 1956, a skeleton had been unearthed by workmen who were constructing a new police house in Wattisfield. The find was duly reported to the coroner by the local policeman and an inquest was deemed unnecessary. Basil was called in and pronounced that the body, which had not been buried in a coffin, was Anglo-Saxon, and that it was possible that there had been a burial ground on the site.

Basil kept a press cutting reporting this find in his notebook which he annotated at various times, including a comment on the original state of the skeleton ("No pelvis & few vertebrae, no teeth.").[13] He also records: "Note: The skull & bones are now in possession of B Brown & stored in shed 1956 & still remain 1965 Dec. 25th." Also, according to Basil's notes, the following year the skeleton was reconstructed, and the skull given to the hospital in Bury St Edmunds!

An inaccurate account

Buried deep in one of Basil's many notebooks is a rather difficult to decipher account of his Sutton Hoo dig. He clearly wrote this some time after the event, and he writes: "Much has been written on the treasure, but little about what transpired at the dig. In some cases, distortion of facts has arisen." Gilbert Burroughs commented: "He did talk on rare occasions about the problems with the excavation and how he was sidelined and walked all over. Everybody else took the limelight, pictures in the papers and so forth, but he didn't moan about it. But I think it did cut very, very deep."

One of Basil's main worries, though, was that the story of this momentous find, and the events surrounding it, should be recorded accurately. This concern came to the fore when, in 1963, Charles Green published his book on the excavation of the Sutton Hoo ship burial.[14] Basil's diary entries in January 1964 reveal that he "went through the Sutton Hoo book by Green as soon as it arrived."[15] The following day Basil Brown records that he has written to Rupert Bruce-Mitford at the British Museum about Green's book ("I differ from some of the information he gives."). Basil was exercised over Green's account of the preliminary work which he believed was inaccurate. Charles Green had clearly not even thought fit to consult Basil: he also gets very few mentions, and then rather grudging ones.

Rupert Bruce-Mitford, however, amply rectified this in his *Aspects of Anglo-Saxon Archaeology*, in which he prints Basil's diary of the 1938 and 1939 excavations (up to the time of Charles Phillips' arrival) in full.[16] Bruce-Mitford says in his introductory note that he felt that this log should be in print somewhere "both as a tribute to an unique Suffolk character and as an essential part of the story of the most remarkable single find in British archaeology." He adds that Basil's "experience and sound instinct was responsible for the preservation of the tenuous structure of the ship."

It was the publication of Charles Green's book that prompted Basil to deposit his diaries and logs relating to his Sutton Hoo work with a solicitor in Bury St Edmunds for safekeeping. It was some years after Basil's death, that the volumes were delivered to the British Museum by Dr Stanley West, in accordance with his will.

Return visits to Sutton Hoo
Basil Brown visited Sutton Hoo again many times after his retirement and when he did so, it was as an honoured guest. No more so than in 1965 when the BBC made a television documentary about the discovery of the Great Ship Burial. A number of those who were involved in the original excavation were interviewed, including Charles Phillips, Stuart and Peggy Piggott, John Jacobs and Basil. Basil was chauffeur-driven from Rickinghall to Sutton Hoo and, as he recorded in his diary, "co-operated in programme of filming site etc. and gave a short description of the mounds excavated in 1938 and finding of the large ship."[17] After lunch at the Bull in Woodbridge,

further filming took place in the afternoon. Basil was filmed walking over the field containing the burial mounds and "everybody seemed pleased."

The following year, Rupert Bruce-Mitford personally invited Basil to see the newly uncovered 1939 Great Ship Burial.[18] He was driven to the site where a detailed plan of the ship was underway. Basil recorded that "a good deal of the lower portion of the ship survived the tanks or Bren gun carriers."[19] Then in his diary in March 1971, Basil recorded that he was made to feel extremely welcome on a further trip to Sutton Hoo to view the final dig of the season by Bruce-Mitford, which coincided with filming by the BBC. He concluded the diary entry by saying that he had tried out his new hearing aid, although sadly he doesn't tell us whether this was successful![20]

A very acute man
In later life, with his broad Suffolk accent, false teeth and hearing aid, many people encountering Basil for the first time might have underestimated him. But anyone who knew him understood that he was nobody's fool. Graham Clayton remembers meeting Basil soon after Graham and his wife had bought Elm Cottage in Rickinghall. He recalled:

> "I came out one day and found this strange elderly figure draped, slightly bonelessly, over my gate. The thing that struck me was that it was quite clear that he had an extraordinary sharpness about him. A very, very acute man. He was very polite, and he asked if he could possibly come in and look at my house. He introduced himself as Basil Brown and said his interest was in local history; he never mentioned Sutton Hoo at all at that point. So, naturally, we invited him in and gave him tea and biscuits and so on, and this became almost a regular fixture, because we would come down about once or twice a month to Suffolk, and when he saw the car, I think he would come round, and we'd have more of a chat. We got into this rather nice ritual where in return for the tea and biscuits we were always given - or loaned I should say - an archaeological notebook, and these we'd take back to London and study with great interest and enthusiasm. They were mostly about the kilns that he excavated in the area. And he was very helpful in telling me a little bit about the early history of my house."

Basil at home in 1969 (Martin Chilvers)

Basil in his front room in the mid-1970s (Peter Christie)

A tradesman's token in the tulips

In his old age, Basil took pleasure in his garden at Cambria. Even then, though, he seemed to unearth something interesting. According to the local newspaper: "While hoeing in his back garden on Friday, local archaeologist Mr Basil Brown, came across a tiny coin near a row of tulips. Most people would probably either not have noticed the coin or would have discarded it, but Mr Brown identified it almost at once as a tradesman's token about 300 years old."[21] Such was Basil's zeal for recording such finds, he even took a photograph of these flowers!

The last dig

"Whilst gazing over the East Anglian landscape, one begins to ponder over the changes the countryside must have undergone since those enigmatic days of prehistoric man; and the changes in man's way of life since that time. Most of us would let the thought drop in a short time; but in the village of Rickinghall one man and his young helpers are doing a lot more than just wondering." This is how Bernard J Fresco started his article in the September 1967 issue of the *East Anglian Magazine*. He was, of course, referring to Basil, this time digging at Broom Hills, a site to the north of the main village. He also seemed to manage to attract an army of youngsters who were eager to learn how to dig for ancient artefacts.

Basil had had his eye on the Broom Hills site for many years. In 1957, he had noted that Roman terret rings (the metal loops on a horse harness) had been found there in 1925 during ploughing. Basil had managed to dig a small, exploratory test pit in January 1960 just after ploughing was completed, where he found what he then believed to be Iron Age pottery sherds.[22]

Basil's full excavation at Broom Hills was to prove his last project, and it began on 5 August 1964 when, according to his diary: "Went to field near Broom Hills to see if there was any chance after the corn had been reaped, of getting a small dig on the hut site, generally thought to be Iron Age but may be late Saxon. Will try to get the sherds in my possession further checked."[23] Basil had to wait a further twenty days before he was able to start digging, with the help of regular helper, John Aves.

Soon, other schoolchildren joined them. One of these was Michael Salt, who said that Basil had time for everybody and liked being with young people: "He'd always talk to you about what he was doing. He'd always give you a trowel and try to teach you something. He was patient beyond belief."

Another boy who assisted Basil at Broom Hills recorded this memory of the dig:

"We were thrilled to be allowed to 'lend a hand'. As young boys, we found the initial stage hard work, for this required the removal of the top layer of soil with heavy spades. Once this had been done, the work became more interesting because we were given small trowels and brushes to scrape and brush away the earth. If we found anything, we would take it to Mr Brown and he would say whether it should be kept or discarded. As we worked, Basil would explain the significance of the different coloured earth and the fragments of pot. We could see how heat had changed the colour of the pots used for cooking and the earth too, where there had been a fire. Mr Brown knew where the walls had been from the earth's colour; we were able to see it too when he pointed it out. We did not find anything really important, but I remember we had fun and were learning all the time."

Over a period of four years, Basil unearthed a large amount of Roman and early Saxon pottery and found evidence, in the form of flint scrapers, of earlier Neolithic occupation. Other significant finds included a bracelet of twisted bronze wire, a bronze bucket handle, green pottery beads, an iron knife and bone spindle whorl. Burnt red soil was found beneath the black soil, together with many burnt bones and sherds of pottery, which led Basil to think that he had uncovered a Saxon cremation cemetery. The majority of the bones, however, proved to be from animals.

Basil also discovered what he described as floors of chalk or lime showing impressions of floor timbers with remains of several hearths. When Basil started out, he had been expecting to reveal an Anglo-Saxon village, but it soon became evident that he had discovered an Anglo-Saxon manor house.

Basil and some of his helpers at Broom Hills (Courtesy of the Compton family)

Basil's tent at Broom Hills (Courtesy of the Compton family)

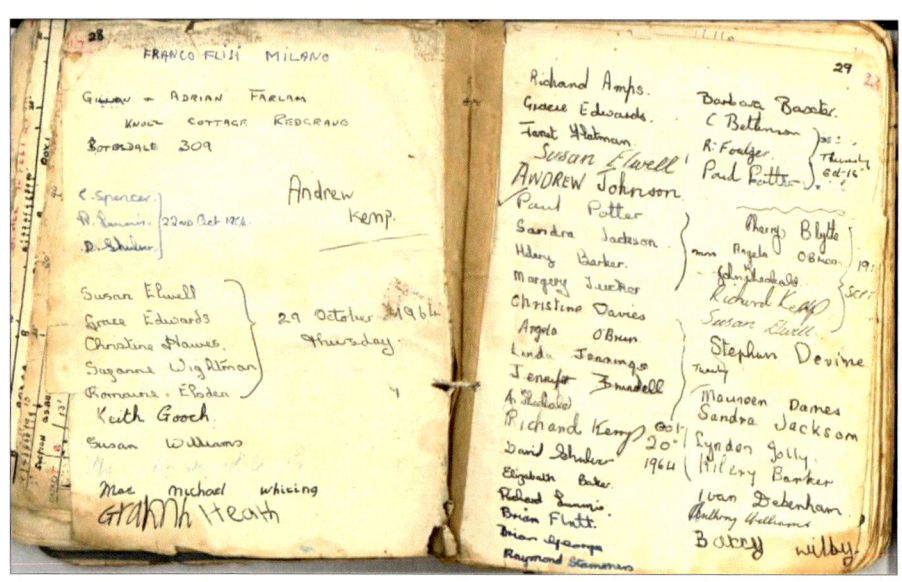

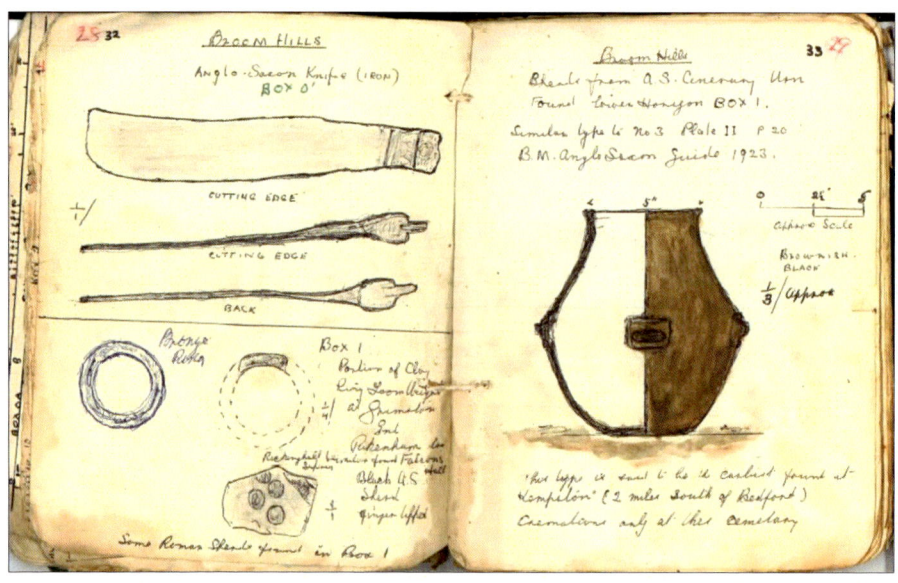

Pages from Basil Brown Archive volume LIII which include signatures of some of the children who helped Basil at Broom Hills (SCCAS)

Bernard Fresco concludes his account in the *East Anglian Magazine* with these words: "Mr Brown is still at work, excavating deeper and deeper into this amazing archaeological freak site and is gradually obtaining more and more proof that his dig is composed of an extremely rare Saxon manor house built on top of an even rarer neolithic causewayed camp."

A momentous year

In the space of just one week in February 1968, Basil received three pieces of extremely good news. The first was conveyed by a visitor who, along with a bottle of wine, brought news that Basil's name now appeared alongside the Sutton Hoo treasure in the British Museum. Then four days later, Basil received a letter from the Prime Minister's Secretary at 10 Downing Street informing him that the Queen had awarded Basil a Civil List Pension of £250 a year in recognition of his services to archaeology. If this was not enough, the following day Basil records in his diary that he received a letter from a London publishing firm explaining that they wanted to reprint his astronomy book.[24]

Such was Basil's obvious pleasure at the Civil List Pension award, that he wrote to a few close archaeological contacts telling them the news. Charles Phillips, with whom he had kept in touch, sent his "hearty congratulations" and Rupert Bruce-Mitford, who had been instrumental in arranging it, wrote back to Basil saying: "I am so glad that we have been able to get this small token of appreciation of your work fixed for you."[25]

In 1970, Basil was informed that this pension had been increased. The offer of consideration of an additional financial contribution to cover any medical costs was also made. A further increase to £500 per annum was made in 1974.[26]

A sort of faint

Basil recorded in his diary for 2 May 1968: "At dig [Broom Hills] working on west side near road. Got quite a lot done and showed further indications of chalk debris which, when developed, may show connections. Mr Lawrence came and I had a sort of faint. He went for the doctor who came and examined me. Dr Richardson took me home and treated my left ear. This may have caused the trouble."

Basil at the Broom Hills dig (Peter Christie)

The following day, Basil wrote: "Dr Richardson called and further examined me. The doctor does not think there is much the matter. I hope there is not but it is better to make sure."[27] These entries demonstrate how Basil downplayed, perhaps optimistically, the medical episode which was, sadly, to end his excavating days. His diary for the rest of the year shows that he largely stayed at home, "unable to do much" and "still not feeling well."

Although we don't have a first-hand account from Dennis Lawrence (who was a local farmer and antiquarian), he later recounted the incident to Graham Clayton who recalled:

"Dennis was wandering around in the village and came across Basil and said to him 'What are you doing now?' and he said 'I'm doing this excavation out at Broom Hills. Would you like to come and have a look?'. Dennis had nothing better to do, so they walked out together to the end of Fen Lane and up the other side a little way and there was the dig. Basil leapt into the hole and started explaining all the various levels in it and what was where and so on. At this point he suddenly stopped entirely and collapsed on the floor. Dennis thought 'This is terrible - what's happened?' so he immediately sprinted back into the village and got to the nearest house that had a telephone, rang and summoned the ambulance and then sprinted back to see if there was anything he could do, to find Basil stood up, looking extremely angry and demanding to know where Dennis had gone, completely unaware that he'd had possibly a mild heart attack or something else quite serious."

Basil's first biographer

When his health allowed, it is most likely that Basil was never idle, albeit confined to his house and garden. In 1968, Martin Chilvers embarked on a remarkable school project for which he was ultimately awarded a "commendable" mark by his Culford School headmaster.[28] Not only did Basil lend Martin many of his notebooks, from which the schoolboy copied notes and sketches, but he also sat with Martin for a considerable amount of time telling him about his own schooldays and earlier life. Martin therefore became Basil's first biographer, recording Basil's own recollections.

The first chapter of Martin Chilver's school project begins:

"After a distinguished career spanning over three decades of excavating, and countless hours of hard, yet patient and often unrewarding, digging Basil Brown has reluctantly been forced to give up his tireless work after having been ill for some time. Happily, he is now recovering but still cannot continue what to him was his life and its own reward … Having to give up his digging must obviously have been a great blow, for though, now nearly eighty, he is still fit. I am sure he will take it in the way he takes everything else and this makes Basil Brown such a nice person to know."

Martin Chilvers ends his project with a rather nice little postscript which reads: "As an example of the growing fame of Basil Brown and the Sutton Hoo treasure is the fact that a Top of the Form question, April 1969, asked 'What did Basil Brown discover at Sutton Hoo?' The schoolgirl gave the correct answer."

An invitation
One local lady who met Basil recalled her first encounter with him, which was with much excitement because she had learnt about his discovery of the Sutton Hoo Great Ship Burial in history lessons at school. After leaving full-time education, she used to deliver bread for the local bakery and described a visit to Basil's house:

"I noticed on the wall a framed invitation to have tea with the Queen, and beside that an oil painting of the dig at Sutton Hoo. I asked what it was like to have tea with the Queen and why he was asked to have tea with her. Mr Brown told me that he was sent the invitation by the powers that be because they felt that he hadn't been properly thanked for all the important work he had done on the Sutton Hoo dig. But he didn't go because of transport problems. Mr Paine in the village did volunteer to drive him down to the Palace, but they weren't going to allow Mr Paine into the Palace to wait for Mr Brown when he had asked them beforehand. So, he told them if Mr Paine isn't allowed to come into the Palace to wait for him after the long journey of bringing him all that way down then neither will he be coming."

This invitation was to both Basil and May and was to one of the Buckingham Palace tea parties to be held on 18 July 1974 from 4-6pm.[29]

Basil and Mr Edwardson, former curator of Moyses Hall Museum, at Cambria in April 1976 (Peter Christie)

Poor health clearly prevented Basil, and therefore his wife, from attending but he nevertheless rightly gave the invitation pride of place.

The new exhibition
Poor health also prevented Basil from attending the opening of the new Sutton Hoo gallery at the British Museum. Angela Care-Evans, then a Research Assistant at the Department of Medieval and Later Antiquities, wrote to Basil on 11 November 1974 describing how the exhibition of the treasure looked well in its new, light and airy surroundings. She wrote: "We have included on the ship panel one of Guy Maynard's photographs of you at work in the prow in the very first weeks of the excavation. You can just see the outlines of the ribs beginning to show up."[30]

It is likely that Basil was never able to visit this new gallery; he either didn't keep diaries after 1973 or, if he did, they no longer survive. He had, however, visited the British Museum in later life and had been made to feel very welcome.

Failing health
In the last few years of Basil's life, he became increasingly frail. In November 1976, May wrote to Peter Christie as Basil, by this time, was no longer able to write himself. She said of Basil: "He is a bit better but just sits here all day and does nothing and does not go out … He takes no interest in anything. Doctor says it is his age."[31]

Basil died at home on 12 March 1977. He was 89 years old. May Brown wrote to Peter Christie describing Basil's last hours, saying:
> "He passed away Sat night at 11pm very peacefully and no pain. Several days he had been unsettled and Sat afternoon he was very unsettled so I went for my faithful friend Mrs Lummas who sent for doctor. This was about 4 o'clock. Dr Cordeaux said he will not be here long. He came back at 8. Basil sat in the chair in a coma. Dr, Mrs Lummas and myself lifted him into bed in the other room and he never moved or spoke. It was chronic heart trouble … I shall miss Basil very much as I have always looked after so much for him."[32] [33]

May suggested in the letter that she would have liked Basil to have been buried in the churchyard at Rickinghall Superior church (where his parents had been laid to rest). However, the churchyard had been closed to new burials; May described it as a wilderness. Instead, Basil was cremated at Ipswich Crematorium on Thursday 17 March. His ashes were scattered on the March Lawn in the New Cemetery and an entry in the Book of Remembrance reads simply: "Brown, Basil John Wait. Died 1977. Remembered with gratitude." The Rector of Rickinghall and archdeacon of Suffolk, the Venerable Donald Smith, said in his address that Basil "had in his lifetime, discovered something which had been of great importance and as long as history was written, he would never be forgotten."[34]

---

[1] The notification of acceptance of his nomination is in Basil Brown Archive volume XCIII (SA/I: HD 3096/1/5). We don't know whether Basil was elected to the Parish Council and, if so, how long he served.

[2] Basil's first few months of digging are recorded in diary entries in Basil Brown Archive volume XCIII (SA/I: HD 3096/1/5).

[3] *East Anglian Daily Times* 20 February 1964. This cutting appears in Basil Brown Archive volume XCIII (SA/I: HD 3096/1/5).

[4] From original drafts of Basil's weekly reports to the Ipswich Museum held at the SCCAS.

[5] Between 1919 and 1921, most of the contents of the muniment room at Redgrave Hall was sold. The bulk of the early material went to the University of Chicago.

[6] This newspaper cutting is held by the SCCAS under Basil Brown Archive volume LXXXVI.

[7] Details, sketches of the ring and location of find, together with several press cuttings are at Basil Brown Archive Card Index No. 1 (SA/I: Acc No 18855).

[8] Handwritten notes made by a member of the SCCAS, taken from Council meeting minutes, are held by the SCCAS.

[9] Basil Brown Archive Card Index No. 1 (SA/I: Acc No 18855).

[10] Ibid. The seal matrix, together with Basil's description of it survive and are in private hands.

[11] Basil Brown Archive volume LXXXIV (SA/I: Acc No 18855).

[12] Basil Brown Archive volume XI (SA/I: HD 3096/1/12).

[13] Basil Brown Archive volume IV (SA/I: HD 3096/1/13).

[14] Green, 1963.

[15] Basil Brown Archive volume LXX (SA/I: Acc No 18855).

[16] Bruce-Mitford, 1974.

[17] Basil Brown Archive volume LXXXI (SA/I: Acc No 18855).
[18] NT SH/BB2/PRIM/DOC/6b.
[19] Basil Brown Archive volume LXXXII (SA/I: Acc No 18855).
[20] In private hands.
[21] *Diss Express* 28 April 1967, page 4.
[22] Basil Brown Archive volume XI (SA/I: HD 3096/1/17).
[23] Basil Brown Archive volume LXX (SA/I: Acc No 18855).
[24] Basil records each of these events in his 1968 diary at Basil Brown Archive volume LXXXII (SA/I: Acc No 18855).
[25] Phillips' letter to Basil is in private hands and Bruce-Mitford's at NT SH/BB2/PRIM/DOC/6l.
[26] Various letters to Basil from 10 Downing Street are kept by the NT.
[27] Basil Brown Archive volume LXXXII (SA/I: Acc No 18855).
[28] In private hands.
[29] This is now in private hands.
[30] NT SH/BB2/PRIM/DOC/6n.
[31] This letter is in private hands.
[32] This letter is in private hands.
[33] Basil's death certificate records that he died from bronchial pneumonia and chronic heart failure.
[34] *Bury Free Press* 25 March 1977, page 20.

Chapter 10
Legacy

"You have come out of it all very well, and will achieve immortality!"

Seven years before Basil Brown's death, Rupert Bruce-Mitford wrote to Basil from The British Museum. Bruce-Mitford was in the throes of writing his multi-volume definitive text on the Sutton Hoo Great Ship Burial.[1] It is a short but extremely poignant letter which reads: "This is just to let you know that I have decided to print your log and diary in full in the big Sutton Hoo publication. It reflects great credit on you and makes excellent reading and shows very clearly all that was done before Phillips arrived. You come out of it all very well, and will achieve immortality!"[2] [3]

Basil Brown Close

The local community in which he lived has never forgotten Basil. In October 1993, Rickinghall Parish Council considered a request from Mid Suffolk District Council for a name for a small, new road off Ryders Way (itself a new estate named after Dr David Ryder Richardson who was a doctor in the village for 33 years before retiring in 1985).[4] The Parish Council suggested Basil Brown Close as the name, which was duly adopted. However, less than a year later, Rickinghall Parish Council received a letter from a resident requesting a change of name of Basil Brown Close. The council voted on the matter and the request was, thankfully, defeated.[5]

Sutton Hoo

In the immediate aftermath of the discovery of the Great Ship Burial, Basil's role in the excavation was, by and large, overshadowed by the academic archaeological establishment. Subsequent digs – led by Rupert Bruce-Mitford between 1965 and 1971, and Martin Carver from 1983 to 1992 – sought to answer more questions, using modern scientific techniques, about the Anglo-Saxon mounds and the communities that created them.

In 1998, following the death of the then owner, Annie Tranmer, the entire Sutton Hoo estate was bequeathed to the National Trust. A visitor centre was opened in 2002, and the exhibitions here and in Tranmer House give Basil Brown and his significant contribution due prominence.

The Sutton Hoo mob
In 1994, the Eastern Angles Theatre Company staged a production written by Peppy Barlow called *The Sutton Hoo Mob* in which Basil Brown was a central character. This comic drama with musical interludes drew out the power struggles between the various archaeological institutions such as the Ipswich Museum and the British Museum, as well as bringing to the fore the tactical leaking to the press of the treasure's discovery. The play was revived in 2006 with performances in community halls, theatres and schools, when it was described as: "A delightful tale of English eccentricity, involving bicycles, prophetic visions, secret hiding places, priceless treasure in grocery boxes and a race to beat Hitler's bombers." The last performances of this second season were at Sutton Hoo.

In 2007, Peppy Barlow wrote a spin-off from *The Sutton Hoo Mob* which was sponsored by the Sutton Hoo Society. It comprised two monologues presented by two actors playing Basil Brown and Edith Pretty. The resulting CD was called *Gold Under The Bed*.

Exhibition
As part of the Open Churches Week in 2007, Jean Sheehan and Di Maywhort, two local historians, organised an exhibition on Basil Brown in Rickinghall Inferior Church. The week-long event (15-21 July) attracted over 300 people. Several information panels on Basil, his life and achievements were loaned from the National Trust at Sutton Hoo. These were augmented by displays put together using information, photographs and other material given or loaned by local people who had known Basil.

The Suffolk Archaeology Unit (now the SCCAS) loaned the organisers several of Basil's notebooks and a first edition copy of Basil's astronomical book was on display courtesy of the British Astronomical Society. Archaeologists from the Portable Antiquities Scheme in Suffolk brought in a handling collection and were present to identify visitors' finds. Many of the people who came to the exhibition had known Basil and readily passed on their memories in written form after the event, some of which have been used in this book.

Jean Sheehan and Di Maywhort at the exhibition in 2007 (Peter Coles)

Angus Wainwright, Revd Chris Norburn, Gilbert Burroughs and Edward Martin, Chair of the SIAH, at the 2009 memorial service (Charles Greenhough)

Memorial

On 30 August 2009, a Basil Brown memorial service was held in Rickinghall Inferior Church. It marked the seventieth anniversary of his excavation of the Great Ship Burial at Sutton Hoo. The Suffolk Institute of Archaeology and History (SIAH), of whom Basil had been an honorary member, marked the occasion by presenting to the church a commemorative plaque. It was designed and made by Gilbert Burroughs in replica Roman Samian ware. Mr Burroughs, a leading expert on Roman Samian ware pottery, had known Basil personally and shared his recollections of Basil during the service at which nearly 150 people attended. The congregation included academics, archaeologists and historians, as well as people who had known Basil.

The congregation on this special occasion was welcomed by the Rector, Revd Chris Norburn which was followed by an introduction by the Chair of the SIAH, Edward Martin. Other contributors to the service included: Dr Sam Newton of Wuffing Education, who read a passage about a royal ship burial from *Beowolf* in Anglo-Saxon; Jane Carr, the General Secretary of the SIAH, who read from the writings of the Venerable Bede, describing how the province of the East Angles accepted the Christian faith; and an excerpt from Basil Brown's diary of his Sutton Hoo excavations read by Angus Wainwright, the National Trust's Regional Archaeologist for East Anglia. Clive Paine, the Excursions Secretary of the SIAH and a lay preacher, gave the address.

It took until late 2012 for the commemorative plaque to be mounted on the north inside wall of Rickinghall Inferior Church: an ecclesiastical faculty issued by the Diocese of St Edmundsbury and Ipswich allowing the installation of this, together with a rectangular brass plaque with explanatory text, had been issued a year earlier.

The Dig

In January 2021, Basil Brown hit television screens across Britain when the streaming service, Netflix, released a film adaptation of John Preston's 2007 novel, *The Dig*. Preston is the nephew of Peggy Piggott, the archaeologist who uncovered the first item of treasure in the Great Ship Burial in 1939. In the book, therefore, John Preston gives his aunt the role of one of the narrators.

Whilst the events surrounding the discovery of the ship and the burial are factual, the novel also uses a degree of literary licence. For instance, Basil's two digs of 1938 and 1939 are merged into one and a completely fictitious character, Rory Lomax, is introduced to add a love interest for Peggy. Lomax controversially takes the place of the two teachers, Mercie Lack and Barbara Wagstaff, who extensively photographed the excavations. Basil Brown is, however, at the centre of the action and is played expertly by Ralph Fiennes in the film, opposite Carey Mulligan as Edith Pretty. The film *The Dig* served to introduce a wider audience to Basil and his achievements.

Blue plaque
There had reportedly been several attempts over the past few decades to have a blue plaque mounted on Basil's former house, Cambria. In 1994, the Heritage Circle – a local history society who meet in Rickinghall – had tried to get a plaque mounted on the house but had met with some local opposition.[6] Both Rickinghall Parish Council and the SIAH had also investigated the possibility of a blue plaque but progress had, sadly, not been made. They were apparently told by English Heritage that, as an archaeologist, Basil Brown was not important enough, and so the institute had, instead, arranged for the replica Samian ware plaque to be presented to the church.

In 2021, Quatrefoil – a small group who research, write, publish and share information on the local history of Botesdale, Redgrave and Rickinghall – resurrected the idea of a blue plaque on Cambria. Sally Green, who as a schoolgirl had known Basil, led the work to contact all the relevant authorities, as well as the owner of Cambria, and established that there were no objections to the project.

On Monday 8 May 2023, exactly 84 years to the day after Basil arrived at Sutton Hoo to begin excavating the mound which yielded up the Great Ship Burial, an excited group of Quatrefoil members gathered outside Cambria to watch Chris Burnard, the owner of Cambria, mount a blue plaque on the house. It reads:

Basil Brown
1888 – 1977
Archaeologist and Astronomer
Discoverer of the Sutton Hoo
Great Ship Burial
Who lived in the village of Rickinghall and in this house 1935-1977

Quatrefoil was absolutely delighted to have such a visible recognition of Rickinghall's most famous resident. Basil is fondly remembered in the neighbourhood by all who knew him, and we are all proud of his many achievements. He was always generous with his time and expertise, inspiring the younger generation's interest in archaeology and local history. Basil Brown did, undoubtedly, achieve immortality.

---

[1] Bruce-Mitford, 1975; Bruce-Mitford, Rupert, *The Sutton Hoo Ship-Burial, Volume 2: Arms, Armour and Regalia* (British Museum Publications, London, 1978); Bruce-Mitford, Rupert, *The Sutton Hoo Ship-Burial, Volume 3: Late Roman and Byzantine silver, hanging-bowls, drinking vessels, cauldrons and other containers, textiles, the lyre, pottery bottle and other items Vol. I* (British Museum Publications, London, 1983); Bruce-Mitford, Rupert, *The Sutton Hoo Ship-Burial, Volume 3: Late Roman and Byzantine silver, hanging-bowls, drinking vessels, cauldrons and other containers, textiles, the lyre, pottery bottle and other items Vol. II* (British Museum Publications, London, 1983).
[2] NT SH/BB2/PRIM/DOC/6d.
[3] In the event, Bruce-Mitford did not include Basil's log and diary in his multi-volume work. Instead, it appears in Bruce-Mitford, 1974.
[4] *Diss Express* 12 November 1993, page 12.
[5] *Diss Express* 9 September 1994, page 39.
[6] Papers held privately record that the objections centred around the fact that Basil had lived in other properties in Rickinghall for longer periods than he had at Cambria.

The Quatrefoil team - Graham Clayton, Di Maywhort, Sue Hardy, Sarah Doig, Sue Emerson, Mike Doig, Sally Green and Jean Sheehan - with the blue plaque (Quatrefoil)

The blue plaque on Basil's former home (Quatrefoil)

Bibliography

Bruce-Mitford, Rupert, *Aspects of Anglo-Saxon Archaeology: Sutton Hoo and other Discoveries* (Victor Gollanz Ltd, London, 1974)

Bruce-Mitford, Rupert, *The Sutton Hoo Ship-Burial, Volume 1: Excavations, Background, the Ship, Dating and Inventory* (London: British Museum Publications, London, 1975)

Carver, Martin, *Sutton Hoo: Burial Ground of Kings?* (British Museum Press, London, 1998)

Clayton, Graham, *Villages in Wartime: Life in Botesdale, Redgrave and Rickinghall in World War Two* (Quatrefoil, Rickinghall, 2014)

Durrant, Chris, *Basil Brown: Astronomer, Archaeologist, Enigma* (Suffolk, 2004)

Green, Charles, *Sutton Hoo: The Excavation of a Royal Ship-Burial* (Merlin Press, London, 1963)

Markham, Robert, *Sutton Hoo: Through the Rear View Mirror 1937-1942* (Sutton Hoo Society, 2002)

Phillips, Charles W., *My Life in Archaeology* (Alan Sutton, Gloucester, 1987)

Skelcher, Mary and Durrant, Chris, *Edith Pretty: From Socialite to Sutton Hoo* (Suffolk, 2006)

Sheehan, Jean, *St Mary's Church Rickinghall Inferior* (Quatrefoil, Rickinghall, 2013)

Watson, F. E., *Culford School: The First Hundred Years 1881-1981* (The Governors of Culford School, 1980)